# The Golf Shot

# The Golf Shot

by MICHAEL W. BIDDULPH

W · W · NORTON & COMPANY
*New York London*

Library of Congress Cataloging in Publication Data

Biddulph, Michael W
  The golf shot.

  Bibliography: p.
  Includes index.
  1. Golf.  2. Swing (Golf) I.  Title
GV965.B548    796.352′3    79–19060
ISBN 0–393–01312–X

1 2 3 4 5 6 7 8 9 0

# Contents

It is a pleasure to acknowledge the following contributors:

COLIN EDWARDS, whose shots from the tee concentrated my mind on the problem of slicing.

FRANK LAMING, whose golf stories kept me amused, and in particular for the 'yard-of-string'.

GILLIAN, for the title.

# The Golf Shot

# 1: Introduction

Golf is played in nearly every country in the world, and its popularity goes on increasing year by year. A recent estimate of the total world sales of golf balls put the number in the region of 150,000,000 per year, most of which are sold in the United States. Even allowing for some awfully bad golfers, this demonstrates the extraordinary popularity of the game. Almost without exception, every one of the millions of golfers is striving to improve his game.

This book has been written to attempt to fill a gap in the literature of golf. Many golf instruction books have been written by successful exponents of the game, all giving tips and hints based on years of experience on the course. However, these books often demonstrate misunderstandings on the part of the authors of the reasons that the ball flies in the way that it does. On the other hand, these reasons are well understood by the authors of many scientific research papers on the subject, but these are too detailed to be of general interest. This book sits between these two extremes, explaining in general terms the effects which cause the ball to behave in the ways that every golfer knows so well. In doing so, many interesting facts emerge, and the reader should gain a better feeling for what he should be trying to achieve with a golf club, and for his chances of success. One of the all-time great players, Jack Nicklaus, recently wrote: 'The reason that most golfers play less well than they'd like—and could—is that they basically do not understand what they should be trying to achieve with a golf club.'

In the chapters which follow we examine in some detail what happens to the ball, from the instant that the club head makes contact, to the instant that the ball stops moving far away down the fairway, or in the rough. In order to do this, and so to attempt to help golfers understand what they are trying to accomplish as they hurl the club head at the ball, we look at the information which has been painstakingly assembled over a period of three centuries. It will come as a surprise to many readers to discover the efforts which have been devoted by some of the world's most eminent scientists, in some cases Nobel Prizewinners, to studies of the humble golf ball. Sir Isaac Newton himself was interested in the swerve of a spinning ball at the time of the Great Plague in 1665.

We shall bring the results of these studies together, from Newton to the present day, and use them to predict exactly the flight path of a golf ball when hit in a variety of ways. In this way we can follow precisely the golf shots resulting from using various clubs, various types of ball (ranging from the old 'guttie' to the modern high-compression ball), various weather and ground conditions, and the position and speed of the club head at impact. Many thousands of mathematical calculations have had to be carried out in order to predict just a single shot. This has only been possible because of one of the wonders of the modern age, the computer. The computer has been programmed to 'play' golf shots under any set of conditions which we care to name, and then to show us by means of a diagram how the shot turned out. Thus we can play shots to our heart's content, and draw conclusions from what we see. The computer, unlike a mere mortal, can always hit the ball in exactly the required way with exactly the required power.

All the shots played and illustrated in this book, except one in Chapter 11, are played with the same power given to the club. That is, the hands are coming through at the same speed for all shots, whatever club is being used. Thus they are 'full' shots, made by a player who could achieve a drive of 250 yards on a firm, level fairway. This is typical of many golfers, although the consistency with which they can achieve such a drive varies considerably from one to another.

The reader needs no scientific knowledge whatsoever to read this book, only an enquiring mind and an interest in golf. For those readers who would like to know more about the methods used, a bibliography of books and research papers is included.

Of course, golf is an art, not a science. However, when we play golf we are always trying to move the club head to the ball within an allowable margin of error in order to achieve a satisfactory result. The only way that we can assess how great is this margin of error is to study the resulting shots in some detail. One of the points of interest which has emerged from this study is the extraordinary accuracy with which the expert golfer moves the club head to the ball. It is a credit to the ability of these players that such control of hand and eye has been achieved.

This book, the 'thinking-man's guide' to the golf shot, will make the game of golf more enjoyable through a better understanding of what is happening, and should lead to better scoring. It should be equally of interest to the expert and to the weekend club player.

# 2: Three Centuries of Study

GOLF IS THE GREAT GAME it is because the ball spins as it flies. The fact that a spinning ball flying through the air travels along a curved path rather a straight line has attracted the interest of scientists over a period of many years. Over three hundred years ago, Sir Isaac Newton realised the importance of spin in influencing the shape of the flight path. In his first published article, in The Philosophical Transactions of The Royal Society of London for the year 1672, he noted the occurrence of swerve in a tennis shot. At that time Newton was Professor of Mathematics at Cambridge University and, at the age of thirty, he sent a communication to the Royal Society describing his remarkable experiments on the wavelengths of light. In speculating that light might consist of a stream of tiny spheres, and wondering why light rays can bend, he observed: '. . . . I remembered that I had often seen a tennis ball, struck with an oblique racket, describe (such) a curve line. For, a circular as well as a progressive motion being communicated to it by that stroke, its parts on that side, where the motions conspire, must press and beat the contiguous air more violently than on the other, and there excite a reluctancy and reaction of the air proportionably greater.'

So Newton had realised immediately that the swerve on the shot was due to the differing pressures on each side of the ball due to the differing relative motion with the air. This is a fact which was not understood by many people centuries after Newton. It is interesting to note that his observations were made in 1665 when he was twenty-three years of age, and that he was interrupted by the outbreak of the Great Plague, which forced him to leave Cambridge for two years.

At the beginning of the nineteenth century, an expert in

4

gunnery by the name of Robins reported that a spinning ball shot from a gun always curved in a predictable way during its flight. He also explained this in terms of the spin imparted to the ball. He even devised a way of demonstrating the effect using a pendulum. His demonstration consisted of imparting spin to the 'bob' of a pendulum and then setting it swinging. He observed that the pendulum started swinging normally, but then gradually developed a circular path as the spinning bob pulled sideways. In spite of this, some famous mathematicians of the time stated publicly that spin could not possibly have a noticeable effect on the flight path of a ball.

The first detailed experimental investigation of the effect was made by a Professor Magnus in Germany in 1852, when he studied spinning spheres in a wind tunnel. Because of these experiments, and the results from them, we now refer to the sideways and lift forces which cause a spinning ball to swerve in flight as 'Magnus Forces'.

In 1893 a Scot, Professor Peter Guthrie Tait, read a paper to the Royal Society of Edinburgh specifically concerned with the flight of golf balls. The paper was entitled 'On The Path Of a Rotating Spherical Projectile', and he followed it with another paper on the same topic three years later. Tait, a Fellow of the Royal Society, was Professor of Natural Philosophy at the University of Edinburgh. Like Newton so many years before him, he had become a Professor of Mathematics at an early age, and it is fair to assume that he hit many a drive onto the fairways of St Andrews. He must have puzzled over the physical laws which govern the way the ball flew, and he was the first to point out that 'underspin' on the ball was responsible for the range achieved by a well-hit shot. This conclusion brought forth heated denials from the golfers of the time,

who felt that this suggestion was a slur on their good cha-
racters as golfers, and that they were being accused of
cheating. Tait seemed to think that the underspin was the
result of a clever 'undercut' at the moment of impact,
rather than, as we now know, the inevitable result of strik-
ing the ball with an angled face club.

Tait made many attempts to measure the speed of the
ball and the amount of backspin at the start of a full drive.
This was in the days before high-speed ciné photography,
and some of his experiments were bizarre in character. In
an attempt to measure the speed of the club head, he teed
a rubber ball 'in front of a horizontal axle on which were
fixed, six inches apart, two large pasteboard discs with
broad borders of very thin white calico. The ball was teed
on a level with the axle, midway between the discs and three
inches beyond their edges. A stout wire, dipped in black
paint, projected from the nose of the club. A drive was then
made, in a direction parallel to the axle; first with the discs
at rest; second, when they were revolving at about nine
times per second'. The paint marks on the discs which
resulted were used to estimate the club head speed, but the
golfer who wielded the club 'confessed that the novelty of
the circumstances had prevented him doing himself jus-
tice!'.

In later experiments he attempted to have a golf ball
driven into a disc of clay, one foot in diameter, suspended
in a doorway four feet away. The golfer encountered some
difficulty in hitting the disc. In order to reduce the risk of
decapitation by a rebound, he surrounded the clay disc with
heavy matting, and he did admit that "the surroundings
were absolutely unlike those of a golf course!". Having
recently attempted to reproduce the same experiment, the
total lunacy of the situation was apparent to me.

Tait also measured, successfully, the rate of backspin of a golf ball by attaching a long light tape to the ball, carefully removing all the twists, fixing the other end to the ground near the ball, and then driving the ball into the clay disc again. The resulting number of twists in the tape enabled him to estimate the rate of spin.

Due to a considerable over-estimate of the upwards force acting on a backspinning ball, Tait speculated that it should be possible to make a golf ball 'loop-the-loop' during the flight of a drive, if sufficient backspin could be achieved. He visualised the side view of a possible drive being of the form shown in diagram 2:1. He was under the impression that the upwards force due to the backspin could be as much as four times the weight of the ball, whereas we now know that this force can only just exceed the weight of the ball. This is perhaps rather a shame, since the drive shown would certainly cause something of a stir among the spectators near the tee.

Before he could complete all the calculations on his golf shots, his laboratory assistant, James Wood, who was labouring over the vast number of arithmetical calculations necessary, gave up and emigrated to Australia. This brought the entire investigation to a halt. Such were the difficulties of scientific studies of the time.

Tait's son, Freddie, inherited his father's interest in golf, and became one of the finest golfers ever produced by Scotland. He won the British Amateur Championship in 1896 at Sandwich, and again in 1898 at Hoylake, but his life ended tragically at the age of thirty when he was killed in action in 1900 while serving with his regiment, the Black Watch, in South Africa. Shortly after, in 1901, his father died also.

In 1910, another Fellow of the Royal Society, the distinguished scientist and Nobel Prizewinner Sir J.J. Thomson, read a paper to the society entitled 'The Dynamics of a Golf Ball'. In his introductory remarks he made an observation which is still partially true today. He said: "If we accept the explanations of the behaviour of the ball given by the many contributors to the very voluminous literature which has collected round the game, I should have to bring before you this evening a new dynamics, and announce that *matter*, when made up into golf balls, obeys laws of an entirely

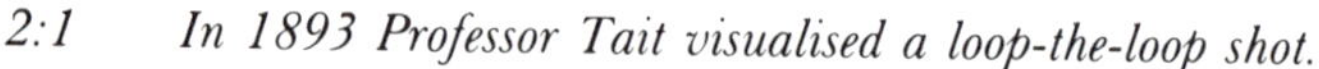

2:1    *In 1893 Professor Tait visualised a loop-the-loop shot.*

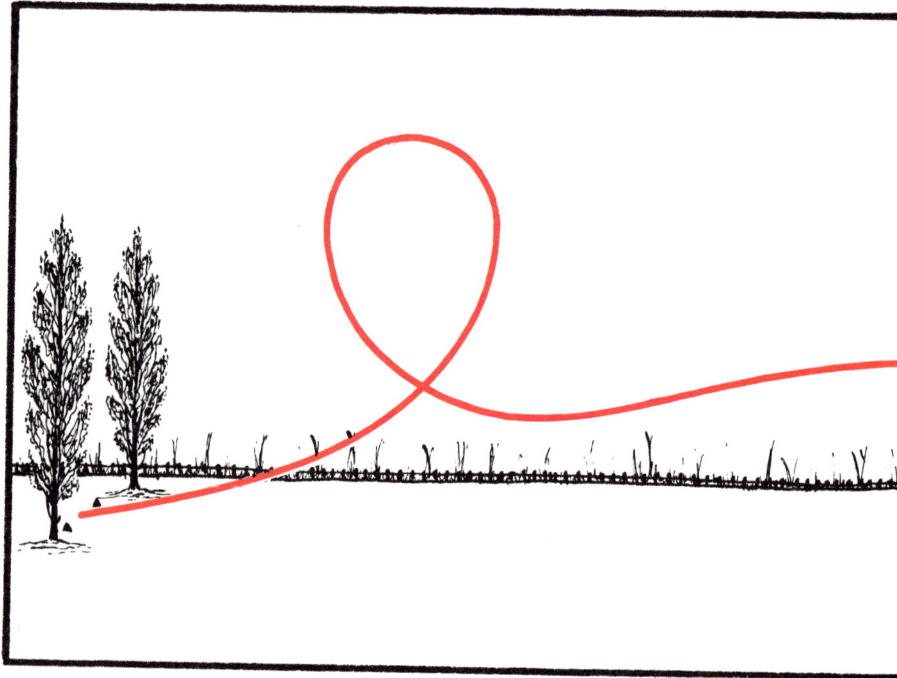

different character from those governing its action when in any other condition!''.

Thomson, like Tait before him, also speculated on the possibility of a 'loop-the-loop' shot, and even went so far as to suggest the likelihood of the shot shown in diagram 2:2. Furthermore, he thought that with enough spin, the ball would go up and fly back over the golfer's head, to land well behind the tee!

Although we now know that it is not possible to produce

such strange behaviour in a golf shot, it *is* possible, and has been demonstrated, using very light, hollow balls. If golf shots like this were possible, who knows what trick shots modern golfers would have perfected.

Other famous scientists who have published papers on the flight of the golf ball include Lord Rayleigh and Barnes Wallis, the inventor of the swing-wing airplane. In recent years several very detailed investigations have been carried out, and these form the basis of the information used in the

2:2　*In 1910 Sir J.J. Thomson suggested the possibility of a multiple loop shot.*

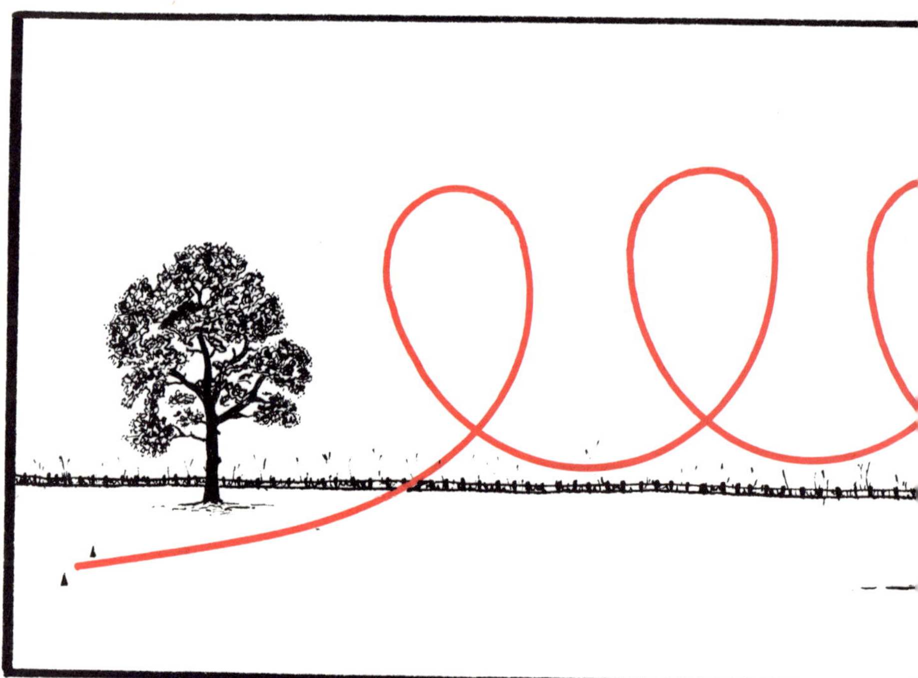

shots illustrated in this book. Some useful information has also emerged from studies of the behavior of baseballs and cricket balls as well as golf balls. The accumulated results of many different people allow us to predict exactly the flight of that little ball which often seems to have a mind of its own.

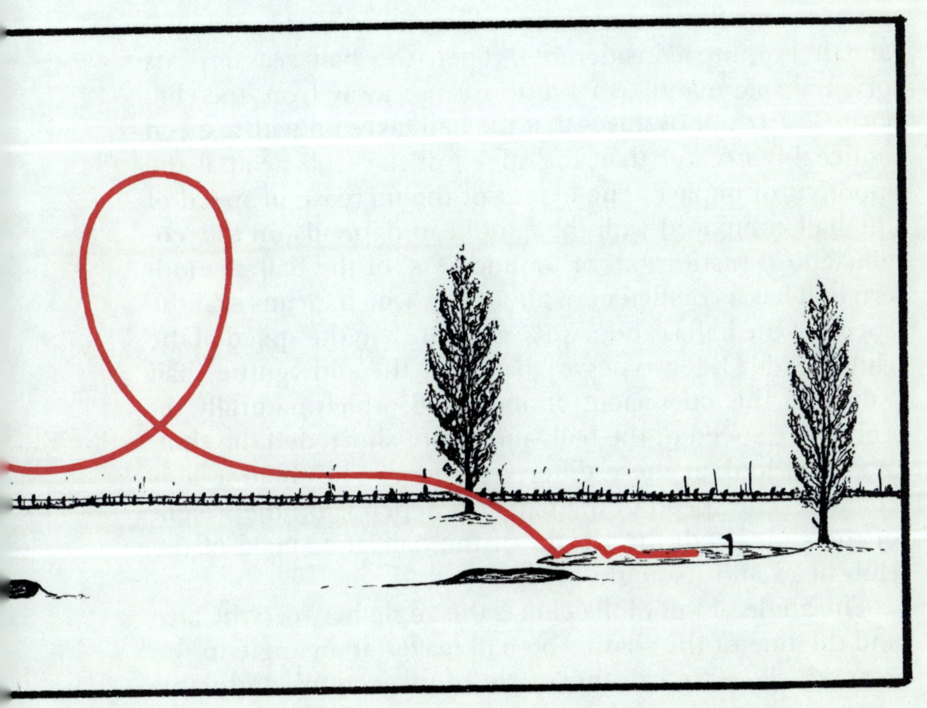

# 3: The Factors Which Influence the Shot

First, consider the influence of spin. If a golf ball were driven with no spin whatsoever under completely calm conditions, it would fly in a precisely straight line towards the target until it bounced and rolled. The bouncing and rolling behaviour would depend on the nature of the ground it encountered. When we strike a ball with the club head, the club and ball are actually in contact for a period of time of less than one-thousandth of one second. During this very short time the ball goes from being stationary to having a velocity of more than 200 feet per second in the case of a drive. This is more than 140 miles per hour.

During the impact, the club face first compresses the ball to some extent and, for an instant, carries the ball along with it. This flattening of the ball is shown in diagram 3:1, and it is quite considerable. Then the ball reasserts its original shape and, as it were, springs away from the club face. The result of this is that the ball takes off with a speed noticeably greater than the speed of the club head at the moment of impact. The extent of the increase in speed of the ball compared with the club head depends on the 'coefficient of restitution' or 'bounciness' of the ball. A modern ball has a coefficient of about 0.7, which means that the speed of the ball is about 40% greater than the speed of the club head. Older types of ball and the old 'guttie' had values of this coefficient of about 0.6, which naturally reduced the speed of the ball, and hence shortened the shot. We shall look at these differences more closely in a later chapter. The speed of the ball also depends on the weight of the club head, the weight of the ball, the speed of the club head and its angle of 'loft'.

The angle of loft of the club is the angle between the face and the line of the shaft. The ball leaves at an angle to the ground which we call the 'angle of projection', and naturally this angle depends on the angle of loft of the club face. The greater the loft of the club, the greater the angle of projection of the shot. This angle of projection can be calculated if we know all the conditions noted above at the moment of impact, and it turns out to be similar to, but slightly less than, the angle of loft of the club.

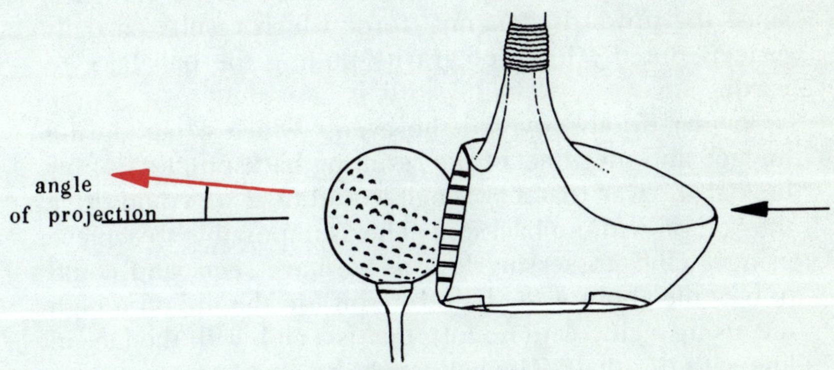



*3:1    The moment of impact.*

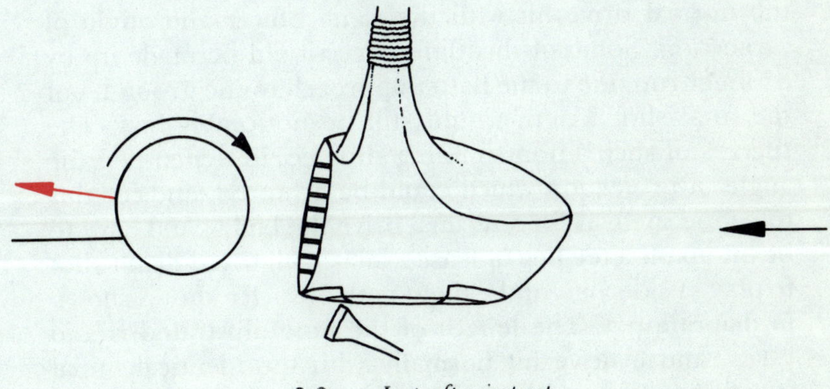

*3:2    Just after impact.*

In addition to being sent off at an angle to the ground, the ball is also given some backspin. The situation just after impact is shown in diagram 3:2. Backspin is inevitable whenever an angled face club makes proper contact with the ball. This is because, during the time that the ball is in contact with the face of the club, it starts rolling up the face, and this is what imparts backspin to the ball. The backspin has a very important influence on the way the ball flies, since the upwards 'Magnus' force which results partially cancels out the force of gravity pulling the ball back to earth.

Having briefly covered the events which occur during impact, and the effect of the resulting backspin, let us now look at the way that a golf ball would fly if we could drive the ball off with no backspin. This is impossible to achieve using a club possessing loft, as we have seen, and could only come about if the ball were hit 'on the up' off a high tee, using a club with no loft, that is a club with the face in line with the shaft. The ball would be acted on by gravity, and the lack of lift force would cause it to dip quite rapidly to the ground, resulting in a carry about 60 yards less than the normal drive hit with the same power and angle of projection. Some of this difference would be made up by a longer run due to the flatter approach to the ground, but the total shot length would still be noticeably less. The success of such a non-spinning shot would depend on the angle of projection which could be achieved, and for this to be the same as for a normal drive the ball would have to be hit up off a tee peg at least 2 inches high, a difficult shot to play. A side view of the flight path of such a shot is shown in diagram 3:3. The length of the hole illustrated is 250 yards, and a drive hit normally with the identical initial velocity and possessing normal backspin would land near the tree and run right up to the pin. The non-spinning shot has pulled up well short of the green.

In all golf shots, the distance achieved before the first bounce, the 'carry', is influenced by another force. This is the resistance due to the air, and is called the 'drag'. The drag, which affects the shape of the flight path, is caused because the pressure of air on the front of the ball is greater than the pressure on the back of the ball. This therefore causes the ball to slow up. The drag is related to the speed of the ball, the drag usually being greater, the greater the speed of the ball. However there is a rather strange effect concerned with drag, in as much as a *CRITICAL SPEED* exists. If this critical speed can be exceeded by the ball, then the air resistance suddenly gets much smaller, in other words the ball will fly further. The critical speed is that speed at which turbulence is created in the air near the surface of the ball. The drag at a speed just greater than the critical speed is about one quarter of the drag at a speed just less than the critical speed, so it is well worth trying to make sure that we can exceed it, and thus give ourselves an advantage. The critical speed for a conventional dimpled golf ball is about 90 feet per second, or about 60 miles per hour. This means that, during a normal drive, the ball is above the critical speed almost all the way.

The reduction in drag on the ball is, of course, a great help, and this highlights one of the reasons for going to the trouble of putting dimples in the surface of the ball. These dimples help to create turbulence in the air near the ball, and so they *reduce* the critical speed, that is they make it easier for us to go faster than the critical speed and take advantage of reduced air resistance. In fact, the critical speed of a ball having a completely smooth surface is about 170 miles per hour and we cannot exceed that even at the

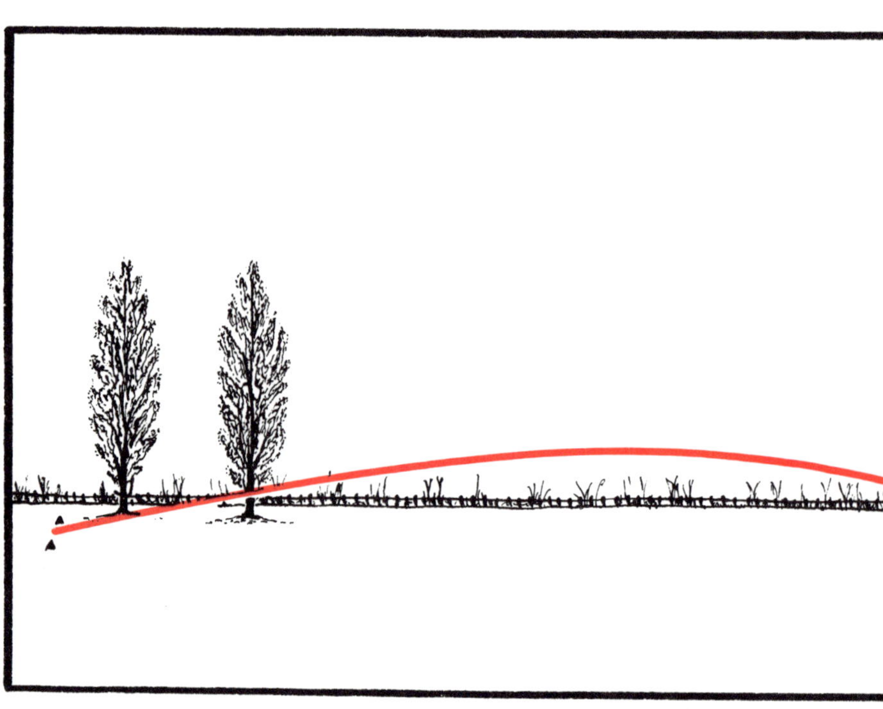

3:3     *Side view of a drive with no backspin. A normal drive hit with the same force would have landed near the tree and run on up to the pin.*

start of a drive. The practical result of this is that if we played the game with such a smooth ball, the air resistance would be so much greater that a full-blooded drive would only carry about 75 yards. This has been confirmed with driving machines, where the equivalent drive with a normal ball would carry 225 yards. Golf would indeed be a very different game if it were not for those little dimples, and their strange effect on air resistance.

A considerable part of the reason for the length of drive normally achieved is due to the backspin which the ball possesses. As we have seen before, this spin introduces a third force in addition to drag and gravity. This is a *lift* force which acts upwards for backspin, and partially cancels out the effect of gravity, especially in the early part of the shot. This is the Magnus force. The three forces acting on the ball as it flies are shown in diagram 3:4, the lift force

16

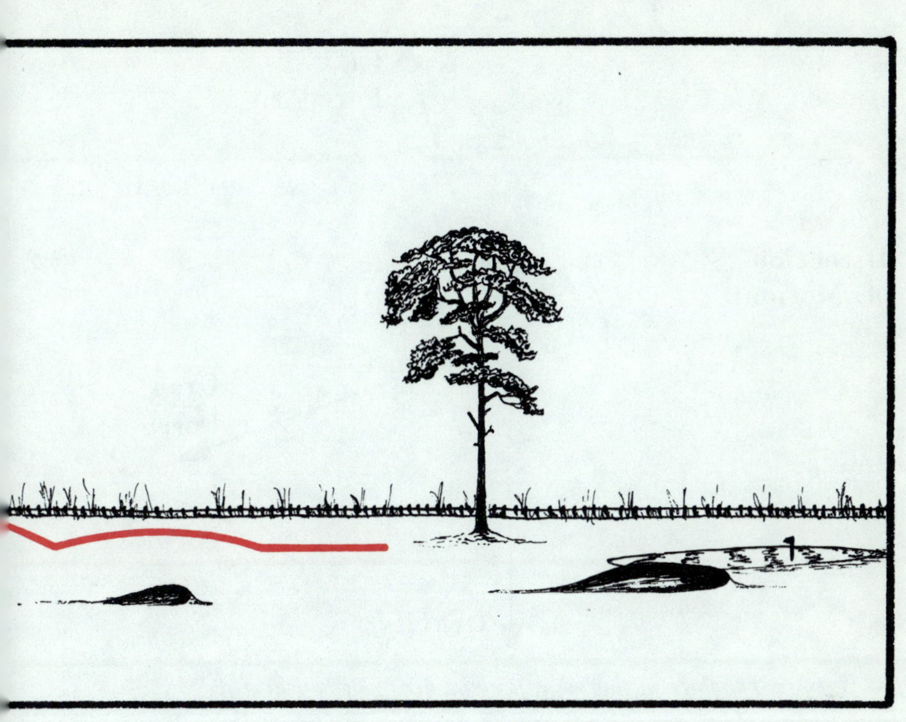

helping us, the drag hindering us and gravity ensuring that the ball does come back to earth.

Briefly, the lift force exists because, in the case of a ball possessing backspin, the top surface of the ball is moving partially *with* the air, whereas the bottom surface is moving partially *against* the air. This difference in surface/air velocities causes an upwards force on the ball due to there being a greater pressure below the ball than above the ball. This pushes the ball upwards. It also has the effect of deflecting the wake behind the ball downwards, as shown in diagram 3:5. An easy way of remembering the direction of the Magnus force is that the ball always tries to 'follow its nose', that is upwards for backspin and downwards for a ball possessing topspin. The dimpling of the surface of the ball has the effect of increasing the lift force, and this is another reason for dimpling as well as the reduction in drag

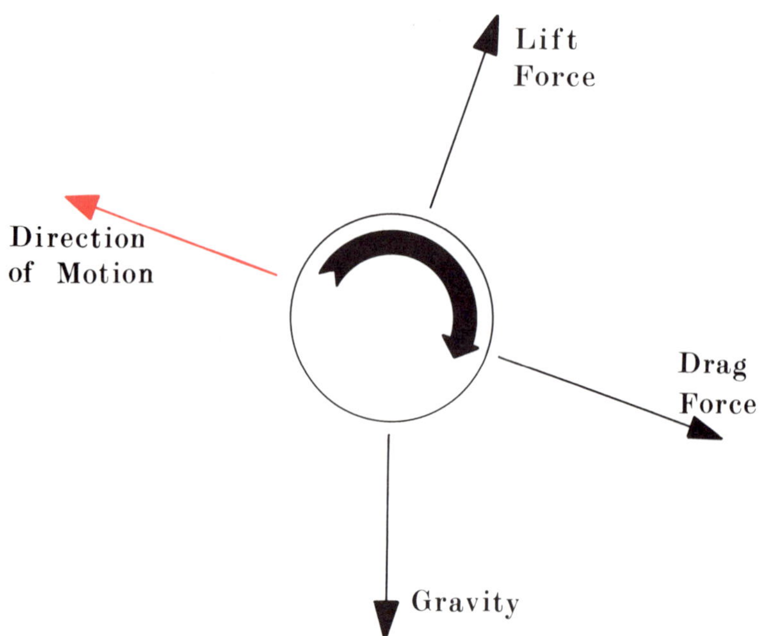


3:4    *The forces acting on a backspinning golf ball as it flies.*

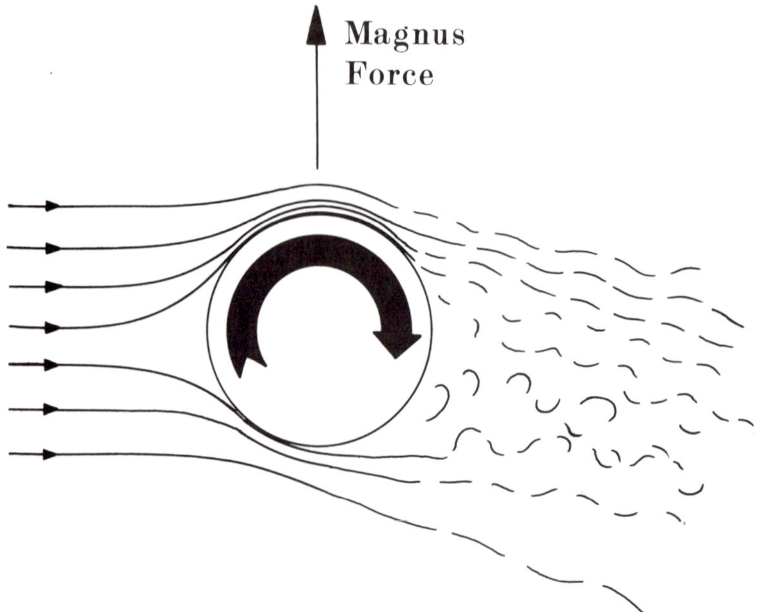


3:5    *Air streamlines near a spinning ball and the deflection of the "wake" downwards.*

18

we have discussed previously. Dimpling will be referred to in a later chapter.

Next, let us consider what makes a ball swerve in flight instead of flying straight. If a golf ball is hit perfectly, the backspin given to the ball will be exactly vertical, that is, it revolves as though on a horizontal axle. This is shown in diagram 3:6 a. This perfectly vertical backspin will be achieved only if the club face is exactly square with the direction of motion of the club head at the moment of impact. In perfectly calm conditions, the result is a straight shot. However, if the face of the club is not exactly square at impact, the backspin given to the ball will not be truly vertical. An element of sidespin is also given to the ball, which means that the ball spins as though on an axle inclined at an angle to the horizontal. If the face of the club is looking to the right of the target at impact, then a sliced shot is the result. This is because the Magnus lift force not only pulls upwards but also acts partially sideways, in this case to the right. Thus the force tends to pull the ball to the right as well as upwards during its flight. This is illustrated in diagram 3:6 b.

Similarly, if the club face is looking to the left of the target at impact, then the force tends to pull the ball to the left, and a hooked shot is inevitable. This is shown in diagram 3:6 c.

This explains why an inside-out swing with a closed face produces a drawn shot, whereas an outside-in swing with an open face produces a slice. In both these cases the face is not square with the line of swing at impact.

We do not always play golf in perfectly calm conditions, much as we might like to. The effects of the strength and direction of the wind on a golf shot can easily be calculated. In this connection it is important to realise that once the

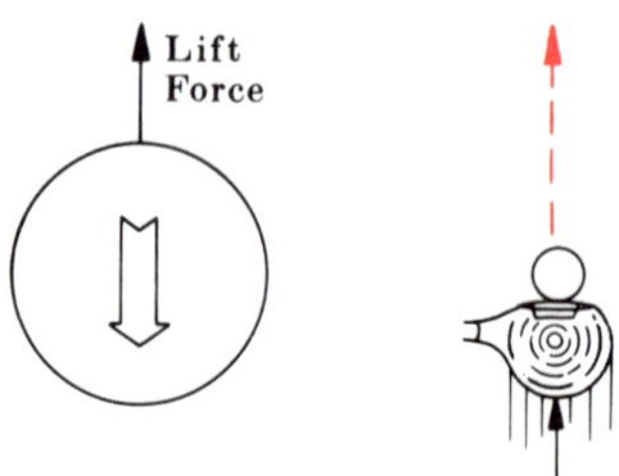

*3:6a    Perfectly hit shot. Vertical backspin.*

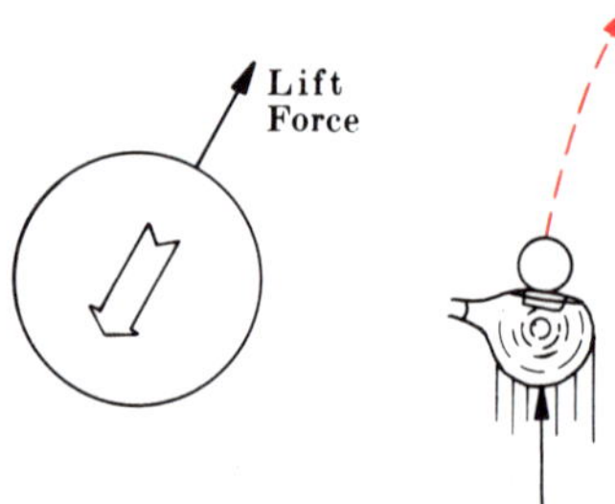

*3:6b    Sliced shot. Angled backspin.*

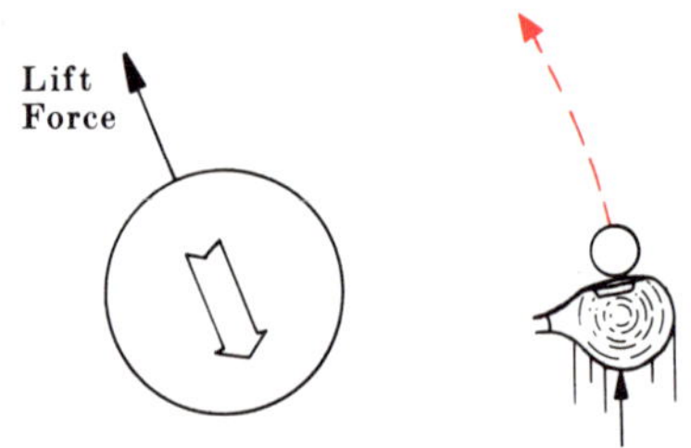

*3:6c    Hooked shot. Angled backspin.*

ball is flying it is only its motion relative to the air which governs its behaviour. The golf ball does not know, or care, whether the air happens to be moving relative to the ground below, and the laws of motion are unaffected. However, we golfers are standing on the ground, and so we see the shot relative to our fixed position. Therefore it is obvious that in order to predict where the ball will land we must allow for the distance and direction of the movement of the air during the course of the shot.

Suppose we drive the ball into a head wind. If we hit the ball with our usual power, in other words the initial speed of the ball is the same as usual relative to the ground, the speed of the ball *relative to the wind* will be faster. In the calculation of speed we must add the speed of the wind to the speed of the ball off the tee. Furthermore, the angle of projection relative to the wind will be slightly smaller than under calm conditions. The result of these changes is that the ball travels somewhat further *relative to the air* since it is going faster. However, we must subtract the distance travelled by the wind during the time that the ball is in the air, and the end result is a shorter drive. The lift force experienced by the ball is greater the greater the speed, thus the drive into the wind experiences a greater lift force and so flies slightly higher. The top of the flight path is also slightly nearer to the golfer as he watches the shot, and this also adds to the impression of a higher shot. This is a small effect though, since the top of the arc is not displaced by much.

A following wind has the opposite effect. In this case the speed relative to the air is reduced, but the length of the total shot is greater by the time the movement of the air relative to the ground is added in. We come across the same effect if we walk along a moving sidewalk. For a given walking speed, we cover a greater distance if we walk with the sidewalk than if we walk against it. Some golfers appear to imagine that the wind actually carries the ball along during its flight. This is not true since the ball is almost always travelling faster than the wind. Even though the angle of projection is slightly greater, the shot is lower because the lift force is smaller due to the lower speed relative to the air.

When we drive the ball through a side wind, we use exactly the same principles to predict the outcome as for head or tail winds. We simply calculate the flight path relative to the air and then allow for the fact that the air has moved across a certain distance during the shot. Naturally the expert golfer allows for the effect of a cross wind on his shot. He might do this by suitably adjusting his target line to compensate, or he may try to hit a controlled draw into a left to right wind or a controlled fade into a right to left wind. The actual effects of playing in windy conditions will be considered later.

Using the principles outlined above, the flight of a ball up to the moment of the first bounce can be predicted with some certainty. However the behaviour of the ball during bouncing and rolling is much more uncertain, depending as it does on the firmness of the ground and the effects of spin on bounce. Experiments have proved that the ball loses little of its spin during its flight, so we have a good estimate of the rate of spin immediately before the first bounce. When the ball goes through its first bounce, one of two things will happen. It may *slide* through the first bounce and come up still retaining some backspin; or it may *roll* through the bounce and lose its backspin in the process. These two possibilities are illustrated in diagram

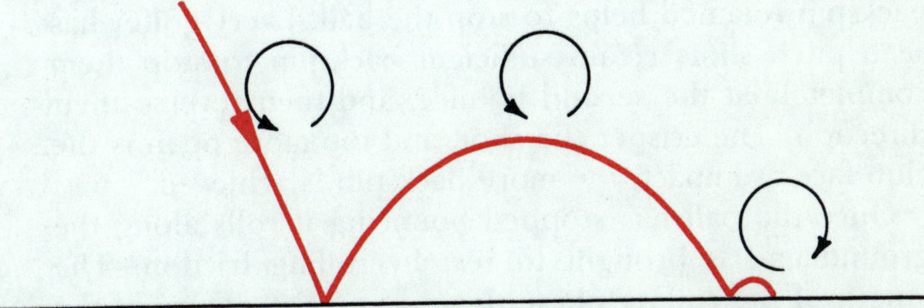

*3:7a    A bouncing ball slides through the first bounce, retaining backspin.
(Reproduced by permission of Hodder & Stoughton Ltd.)*

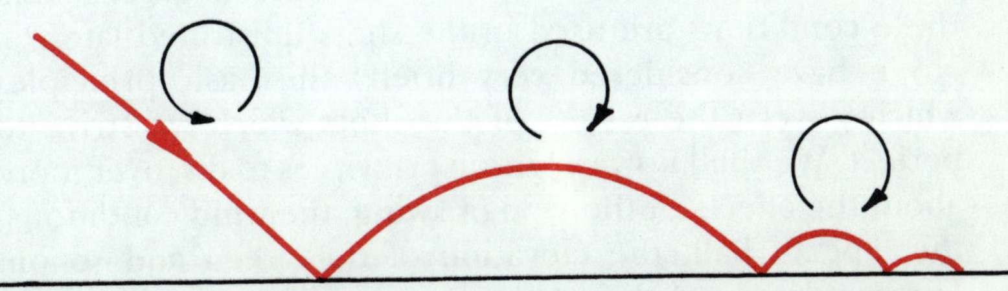

*3:7b    A bouncing ball rolls through the first bounce, losing backspin.
(Reproduced by permission of Hodder & Stoughton Ltd.)*

3:7. In the second case, the ball subsequently has topspin
which makes the run longer.

We usually find that the wood shots and long iron shots
roll through the first bounce because of their angle of approach to the ground and lower rates of spin. The short
iron and pitch shots slide through the first bounce and the

backspin retained helps to stop the ball. Every golfer has seen pitch shots retain sufficient backspin to stop them completely at the second bounce, and then reverse their direction. The crisper the shot, and the more open is the club face at impact, the more backspin is achieved.

Once the ball has stopped bouncing it rolls along the ground and is brought to rest by rolling friction. The length of the rolling phase depends on the nature of the surface.

Because of the uncertainties in the calculations of bounce and run caused by variation in ground conditions, these are not considered in great detail in this book. However, experiments have been carried out on the conditions existing in good firm fairways and on well-watered greens, and these conditions are used in the shots illustrated later.

We have considered very briefly the basic principles which govern the results of the shots which we strive to perfect. We shall now use these principles to discover more about the effects of the type of swing, the wind conditions, the type of ball, the elevation of the green and so on. Further details of the methods are available in the works listed in the bibliography.

# 4: Some Good Shots—and Some Bad

NOW THAT WE HAVE ESTABLISHED THE METHODS which can be used to predict golf shots, we can play a variety of shots and illustrate the results. So many mathematical calculations are required to play just one shot that it only becomes feasible if we can use a computer.

The way that the shots were played was to calculate the position, speed and direction of the ball at successive time intervals of one-fiftieth of one second from the moment the club head hit the ball to the moment that the ball stopped rolling along the ground at the end of the shot. The total duration of a shot could be as much as 14 seconds, and so this involved calculating all the conditions as many as 700 times for a single shot. Each one of the 700 positions involved about 80 different calculations, and so the computer might make as many as 56000 calculations in playing a single shot.

If Professor Tait's laboratory assistant had attempted to achieve this in 1890 by sitting at a desk and calculating by hand, it could well have taken him six months, provided that he could have kept going eight hours a day, and worked weekends as well. The computer does it in 1 1/2 seconds of furious activity, which is about one-tenth of the time the actual ball would take over the same shot. This gives some idea of the way that computers can help us to make staggeringly large numbers of calculations and to achieve results which would have been completely impossible formerly.

When the computer has finished its work we have a column of numbers which tell us exactly where the ball is at any instant, and also how fast it is moving and in which direction it is travelling. With this information at hand we can draw out the flight path of the ball in a number of different ways. Firstly we can draw the 'golfer's eye view' of the shot, that is the view that the golfer has of the ball as it heads off towards the target. For this view we assume that the golfer is right-handed and is six feet tall. This view is the most interesting one, and it is the one which will generally be used to illustrate the shots.

We can also give a side view of a shot, that is as it would appear from an observation point well away to the side of the fairway. This view shows the shape of the arc of the shot. We can also show how the shot would appear from a helicopter high above the course, and this view shows up any draw or slice. Finally we can show a 'caddy's eye view' from behind the flag as the shot comes in.

First of all we will play the absolutely perfect straight drive. The weather is calm and still, and the shot never deviates a fraction of an inch as it wings its way to the target. The golfer's eye view is shown in diagram 4:1. This perfect shot was hit with a driver having a loft of 12 degrees, off a tee peg about 1/4 inch above the bottom of the arc of the swing. In other words the ball was hit very slightly 'on the up'. The club head was moving through the ball at a speed of 164 feet per second, that is about 113 miles per hour. This is fairly typical of a reasonably good golfer. We can see from diagram 4:1. the fact that the right handed golfer who played the shot was standing about two feet from the ball as he hit it.

Diagram 4:2. shows the side view of the same shot. We can note some interesting features of the golf drive from this view. The first part of the shot is almost straight. The reason for this is that the lift forces due to the backspin are almost cancelling out the efforts of gravity to pull the ball downwards. Then as the air resistance slows the ball, the lift forces get less even though the ball is spinning at almost the same rate as when it started. Thus the ball reaches a maximum height, in this case about 69 feet, after 2 1/2 seconds and 131 yards out from the tee. The ball continues to slow and gravity gets a stronger and stronger grip. It falls towards the ground at an ever increasing angle, and actually begins to speed up again as it hits the fairway. It strikes the ground at a speed of 53 1/2 miles per hour and an angle of 38 degrees to the horizontal. The ball was revolving at 57 revolutions per second throughout its flight, and it left the tee at a speed of 157 1/2 miles per hour. We can see that the air has slowed it considerably.

4:1     *The golfer's view of a perfectly straight drive.*

The carry (the distance of the first bounce from the tee) is 203 1/2 yards, and the ball has taken 5 1/4 seconds to get to this point. The ball rolls through its first bounce, which destroys all its backspin and gives it some topspin. The fairway is assumed to be hard, perhaps typical of conditions on a links course. This means that the ball bounces up to a height of 8 1/2 feet and bounces again 18 yards further on. Three more bounces take it another 16 yards and then it rolls 12 yards before coming to rest almost 10 seconds after it was hit. The total length of the drive is 249

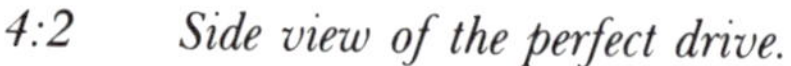

4:2    *Side view of the perfect drive.*

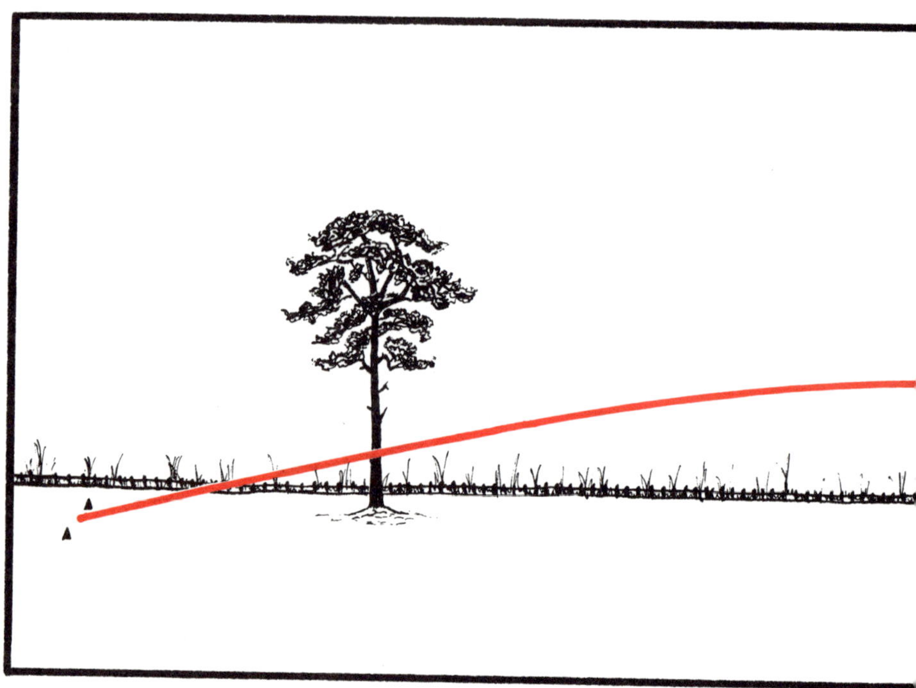

1/2 yards, which is typical of a good player into a firm well-mowed fairway. The distance agrees well with tests made using golf-driving machines, and the shape of the flight path has also been confirmed by careful observation. Naturally, if the fairway was softer and more holding the bounce and run phase would be considerably reduced.

Driving machine tests have also shown that the length of the shot is almost directly proportional to the speed of the ball off the tee, so if we could increase the speed off the tee by 50%, then the drive would be about 50% longer.

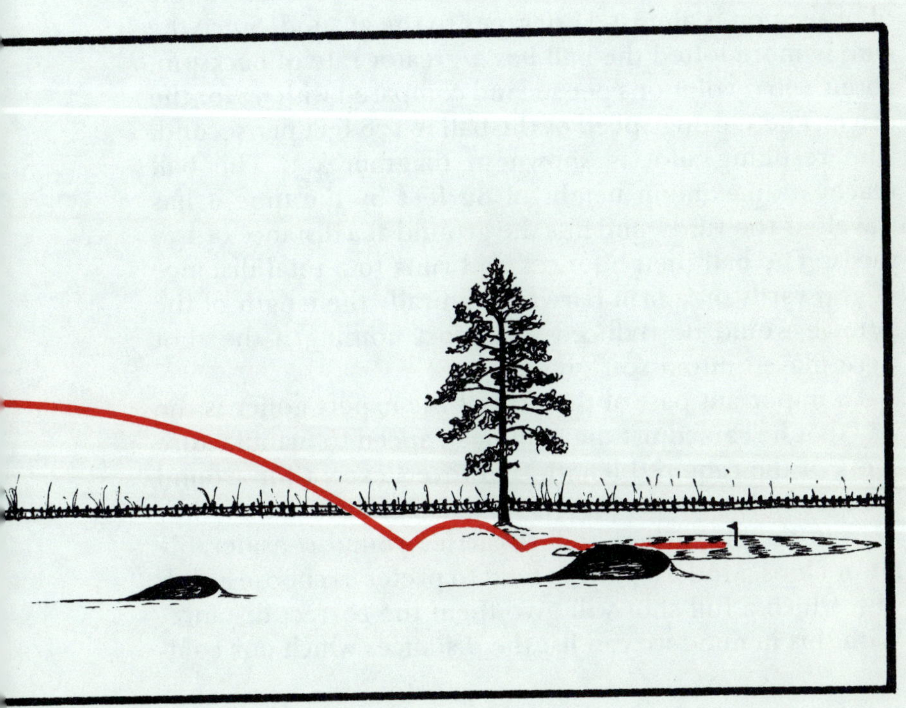

The perfect shot we have just played is rare indeed. However let us play a similarly perfect shot with a middle iron, say a 5-iron. This club has an angle of loft of 26 1/2 degrees. Another difference between the 5-iron and the driver is in the length of the shaft, in this case it is nearly six inches shorter. One result of this is that the club head speed through the ball is slower than in the case of the drive even if the hands come through at the same speed in both cases. Thus a full 5-iron would generate a club head speed of 141 feet per second, about 96 miles per hour, compared with 113 miles per hour in the case of a drive. The shot is hit from a fairway lie, so the angle at which the ball takes off is somewhat less than the loft of the club. Thus the angle of projection is almost 21 degrees to the ground. Since the club is more lofted the ball has a greater rate of backspin, about 100 revolutions per second compared with 57 for the drive. The starting speed of the ball is 178 feet per second. The resulting shot is shown in diagram 4:3. The ball reaches a maximum height of 82 feet by the time it has travelled 100 yards, and hits the ground at a distance of 158 yards. The ball then bounces and runs to a total distance of 189 yards on a firm fairway. Naturally the length of the bounce would be reduced to almost nothing if the shot were played into a soft green.

An important part of the skill of the expert golfer is the way that he can adjust the club head speed to manufacture shots of the required length. However, except for around the green, these 'half shots' are less common now than they were in the days when golfers carried round considerably fewer clubs. Modern players tend to prefer to choose a club with which a full shot will give them the correct distance. With this in mind we can list the distances which our com-

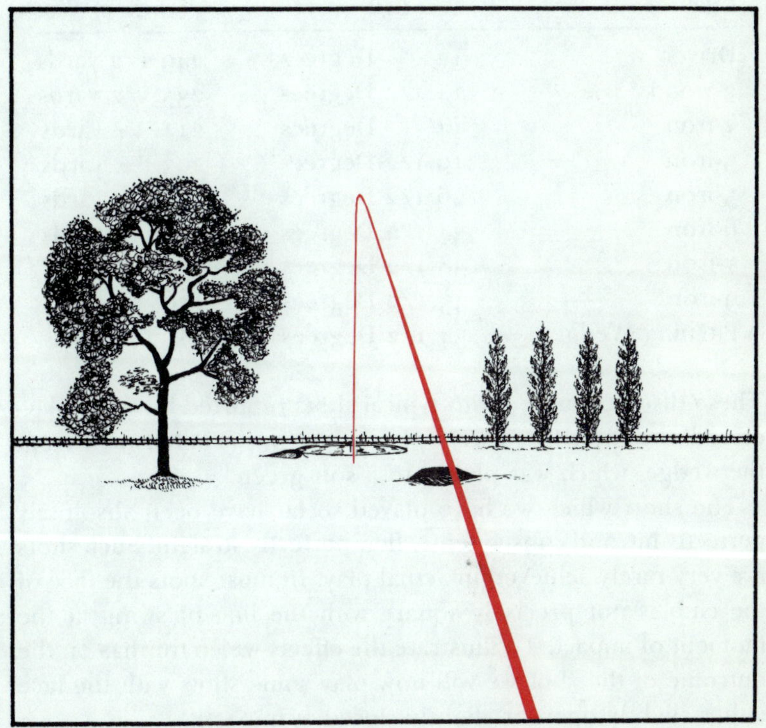

*4:3*     *The golfer's view of a perfectly straight 5-iron shot.*

puter achieves with a selection of clubs, supposing they are all full shots, that is the hands are coming through at the same speed for all shots. We also list the loft of the clubs used, since different manufacturers' clubs of a particular number can be different from one another. All shots are played from a fairway lie except the driver, which is a teed shot.

| Club | Loft | | Length of Shot | |
|------|------|--|----------------|--|
| Driver | 12 | Degrees | 249 1/2 | yards |
| 3-wood | 14 1/2 | Degrees | 235 1/2 | yards |
| 2-iron | 14 | Degrees | 211 | yards |
| 3-iron | 19 1/2 | Degrees | 203 | yards |
| 5-iron | 26 1/2 | Degrees | 189 | yards |
| 6-iron | 34 1/2 | Degrees | 171 | yards |
| 7-iron | 38 1/2 | Degrees | 154 | yards |
| 9-iron | 43 1/2 | Degrees | 119 | yards |
| Pitching Wedge | 54 1/2 | Degrees | 81 | yards |

These distances agree with typical shots reported by good players. All the shots listed were played into our firm fairway except the wedge, which was played to a soft green.

The shots which we have played so far have been absolutely perfectly hit, and consequently flew perfectly straight. Such shots are very rarely achieved in actual play. In most shots the face of the club is not precisely square with the line of swing at the moment of impact. To illustrate the effects which this has on the outcome of the shot we will now play some shots with the face either slightly open or slightly closed at impact.

## CLUB FACE OPEN

In this situation, for the right-hander, the face of the club is looking slightly to the right of the line of swing, which, if we are aiming straight for the flag, means to the right of the target. This has four main effects on the result:

a)   It increases the effective loft of the club by a predictable amount.

b)   It increases the amount of backspin given to the ball, thus increasing the lift force on the ball.

c) It means that the backspin given to the ball is inclined at an angle to the vertical instead of being true backspin. This was shown in diagram 3:6 b.

d) The ball is sent off at an angle to the right of the swing line, the line to the flag.

If the club face is opened by a given angle, then the magnitude of the above effects can be predicted by carefully considering the events which occur during the split second that the club and ball are in contact. We find that the effects depend not only on the amount by which we open the club face, but also on which club we happen to be using.

The increased angle of projection and the greater rate of backspin both lead to a noticeably higher flying shot. In addition, the fact that the Magnus force is pulling upwards at an angle to the right means that there is a continuous sideways pull on the ball, resulting in the familiar slicing shot. The continuing pull on the ball to the right leads to the familiar effect of the slice getting worse and worse as the shot progresses. In many of these shots the ball seems to be going reasonably well for quite a considerable distance, and it is almost possible to convince ourselves that it will all turn out alright after all. Then the inevitable happens and the ball seems to veer sharply to the right. This is partly due to the increasing angle to the target line, but it is also partly an optical illusion. Because the right-hander is standing to the left side of the ball, looking towards the flag, as he hits it, the ball comes into his field of view from the right as he gazes hopefully down the fairway. This is why the golfer's view of the straight drive appears as it does (diagram 4:1). Therefore the sliced drive starts off moving across our field of view from right to left, but fairly soon this apparent motion is reversed and the ball moves from left to right. This reversal of apparent motion usually occurs near the top of the arc of the shot. The optical effect contributes to the initial feeling that the shot may be reasonable, followed by the familiar deepening depression as the ball makes off towards the rough. The whole thing is made worse by the fact that the ball starts off at a slight angle to the right anyway. We can illustrate a reasonably severe example by opening the face of our driver by 10 degrees and watching the result. This shot is shown in diagram 4:4. We have given ourselves some real problems for the next shot to the green. The ball has finished all of 93 yards to the right of the intended target, and is over 20 yards short of being pin-high. This illustrates clearly the severe penalty of not keeping the club face square with the target line at impact.

If we could have positioned ourselves high over the course while this type of shot was played, it would appear as shown in diagram 4:5. Here we can see the start to the right, and then the gradually increasing angle as the shot progresses. Comparing this with diagram 4:4, both exactly the same shot, shows the optical illusion at work. The shot was hit with precisely the same club head speed as for our earlier perfect straight shot.

## CLUB FACE CLOSED

Here the club face is looking somewhat to the left of the target line. The equivalent effects are:

a) It reduces the effective loft of the club by a predictable amount.

b) It reduces the amount of backspin on the ball, reducing the lift force.

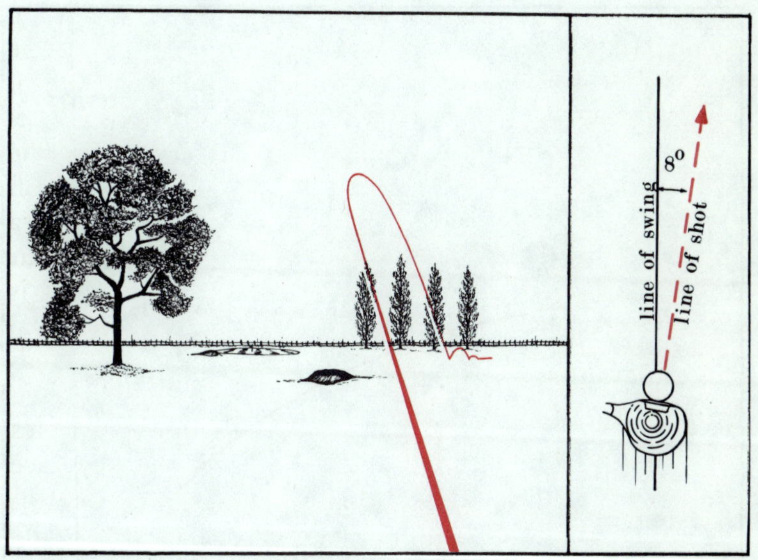



*4:4     A sliced drive hit with the club face open by 10 degrees.*

c) The ball spins at an angle to the vertical, similar to the situation shown in diagram 3:6 c.
d) The ball starts at an angle to the left of the line to the target.

As in the case of the slice, these four effects conspire to exert a considerable, and generally unwelcome, influence on the shot. A hook or draw results. The first two effects cause the shot to fly lower with a shorter carry. The flat approach to the ground does result in a longer run phase. The last two effects create the tendency to start left of the target and then get steadily worse all the way.

The optical illusion works in the opposite way compared with the slice. This time the ball is moving across the

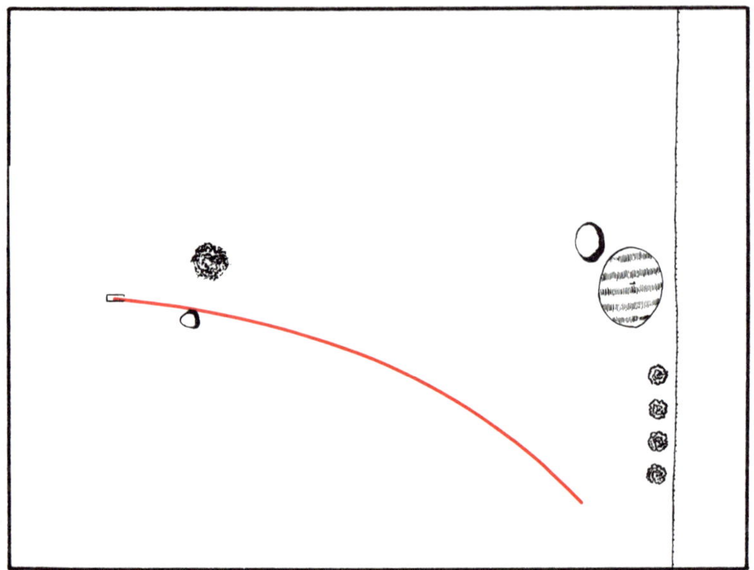

4:5    A bird's eye view of the drive shown in 4:4.

golfer's field of view from right to left throughout the entire duration of the shot. This means that the ball tends to nip quickly across, skulking away to the left and sometimes threatening to demolish the Pro Shop. We do not see the same delayed action effect since the ball is moving right to left the whole way.

The shot which we will now play is hit with exactly the same power as the earlier drives, but the club face is closed by 10 degrees so that it is looking slightly to the left of the target line. The ball takes off with a lower trajectory, 9 1/2 degrees to the horizontal compared with 14 1/2 degrees for the perfectly hit straight drive. In addition, the ball starts on a line nearly 8 degrees to the left of the intended line. The track of the shot is shown in diagram 4:6. This is a familiar shot for the golfer who has a natural tendency to draw the ball from right to left, and sometimes produces a snorter. The shot reaches a maximum height of only 27 1/2 feet, and achieves a carry of 152 yards, the first bounce occurring after a time of only 3.1 seconds. However, the fact that the ball hits the ground at high speed and at a shallow angle, about 19 degrees to the horizontal, means that the bounce and run phase of the shot is longer than usual. If the bounce and run is all along a firm fairway, the shot ends up only slightly shorter than the perfect straight drive. However, since the ball has gone well off to the left of the target, it would normally have run into trouble. If the

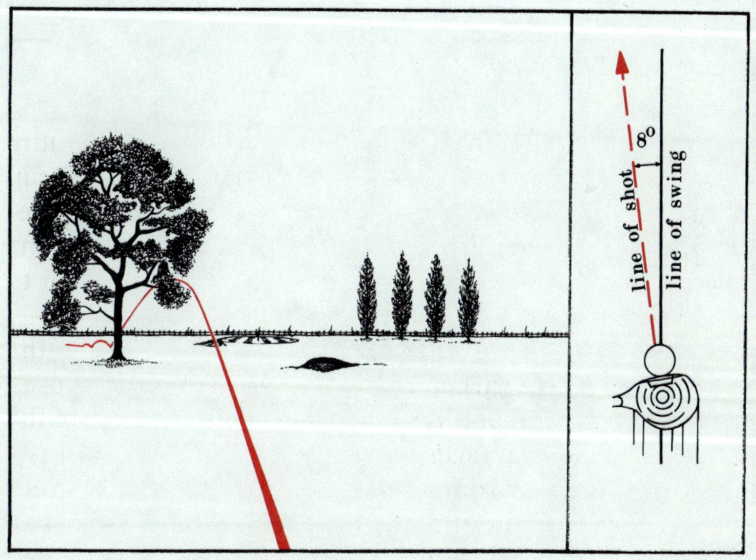


*4:6     A hooked drive hit with the club face closed by 10 degrees.*

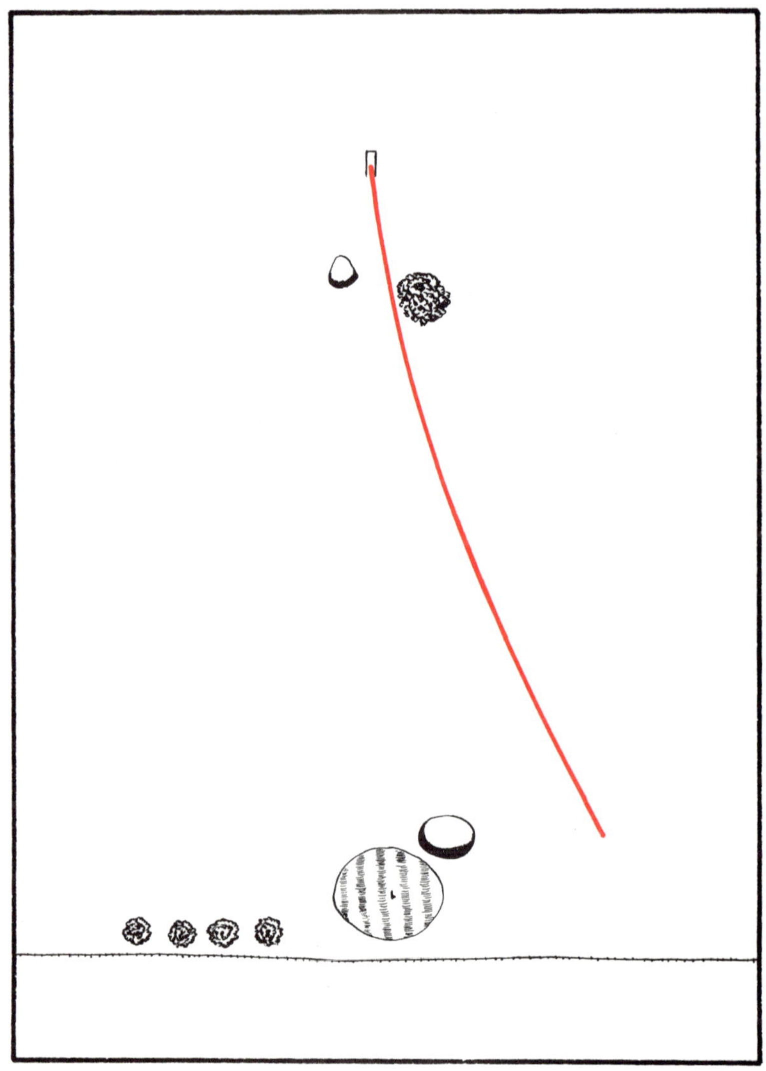

4:7    *A bird's eye view of the drive shown in 4:6.*

shot could have run its course in fairway conditions it would have finished 85 1/2 yards off line, not quite as far as the equivalent slice. The reason for this is that the slice spends longer in the air and the sideways force has a greater time to exert its influence.

A bird's eye view of a similar hooked drive is shown in diagram 4:7. This is not as disastrous as the slice shown earlier on the same hole, but is still not the ideal drive.

The ultimate influence of either opening or closing the club face will be greater, the smaller the angle of loft of the club being used. This is because the important factor is ratio of the "angle-off-square" to the "angle-of-loft". This is the reason that the woods are much more likely to give badly sliced or hooked shots than the middle irons. In other words we have a much smaller available margin of error when using the woods than when we are using more lofted clubs. This agrees with experience in actual play, and it adds to the feeling of apprehension felt by many golfers as they stand on the tee. It also adds to the feeling of great satisfaction when we do hit a drive straight down the middle.

By playing a series of drives with gradually increasing angles off square at impact with a 1-wood, we can illustrate the magnitude of the effect on the shot. The most important effect from the golfer's point of view is the distance off line that the ball finishes, since this will determine whether the shot hits trouble. The relationship between this distance and the angle off square at impact is shown in diagram 4:8. We can see from this graph that, for example, the club face has only to be open by 1 degree to result in a shot ending 35 feet off the intended line. An angle of 1 degree is shown in diagram 4:9. This clearly illustrates the extraordinary accuracy with which the really good golfer controls the club head as it comes through the ball, and it shows why so much practice is required to develop a grooved and reproducible swing. If we could throw a pebble with the same order of accuracy and consistency we would be able to hit a small tin can at a distance of thirty feet with every single throw, the equivalent of a 1 degree angle within which the throw must be made.

For lesser mortals a really wild drive occurs occasionally. Before leaving the 1-wood shots we will play such a drive. Here the golfer has lost control of the club and has unintentionally opened the face by 20 degrees. The shot flies high and wild, over the fence and far away. Remember that the swing line was accurately towards the flag. The shot is shown in diagram 4:10. Small wonder it is not uncommon to see golfers move off from the first tee, head down, and make for the out of bounds markers.

On a more optimistic note, if we can hit our drive with the face 3 degrees open at impact, shown in diagram 4:11, then a much less disastrous and frequently hit shot results. The golfer's view of this shot is shown in diagram 4:12.

The important differences between the wooden clubs and the irons are that the irons are shorter and the club heads have greater amounts of loft. The shorter shaft lengths result in slower club head speeds through the ball even if the hands come through at the same speed. This is the way that most golfers try to play, that is using the same swing speed for all clubs and allowing the choice of club to govern the length of the shot. The greater loft of the club results in a higher, shorter shot, with the ball having greater backspin. This extra backspin results in the lift forces on the ball being greater and a shorter bounce and run phase.

The greater loft of the club also means that the club is

more tolerant of the face being out of square with the line of swing at the moment of impact. As we have seen earlier the important value is the ratio of the "angle-off-square" to the angle of loft; this ratio will naturally be smaller for a club with greater loft. This is the explanation for the common observation that slice or hook in middle or short iron shots is less severe than for the woods or long irons.

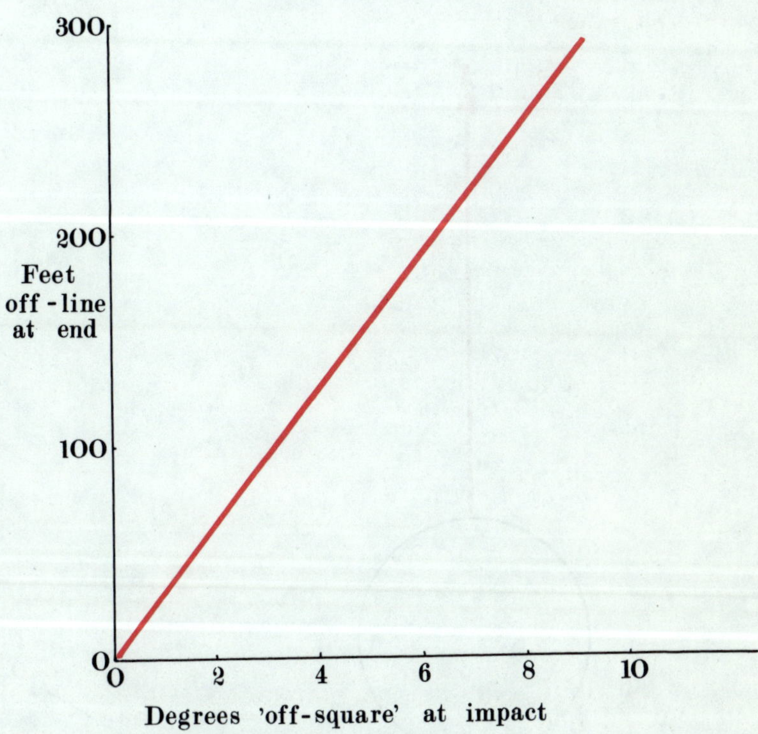


4:8    *The relationship between the club face "angle-off-square" and the distance off line at the end of the drive.*

We shall illustrate the middle iron shots by playing some 5-iron shots. First the perfect 5-iron shot, shown in diagram 4:13. The length of this shot is 189 yards, the perfect recovery after a bad drive on the hole shown.

Now for a noticeably sliced shot with a 5-iron. The line of swing is accurately lined up on the target, but we have opened up the club face by 10 degrees. The ball takes off

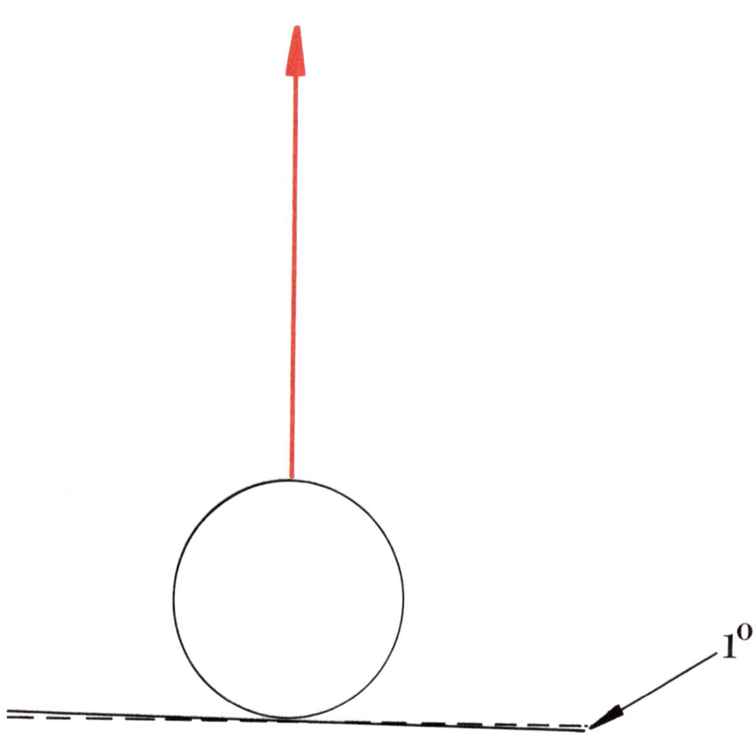


4:9    *An illustration of a club face open by one degree at impact.*

with a speed of 164 feet per second for our 'full' shot, and with an angle of projection of 24 degrees to the ground. The rate of backspin is 115 revolutions per second, compared with 57 revolutions per second for a 1-wood shot. The golfer's view of the shot is shown in diagram 4:14. If we compare this shot with the 1-wood shot shown in diagram 4:4, we can clearly see how the 5-iron has given a much less disastrous result, even though the club head was

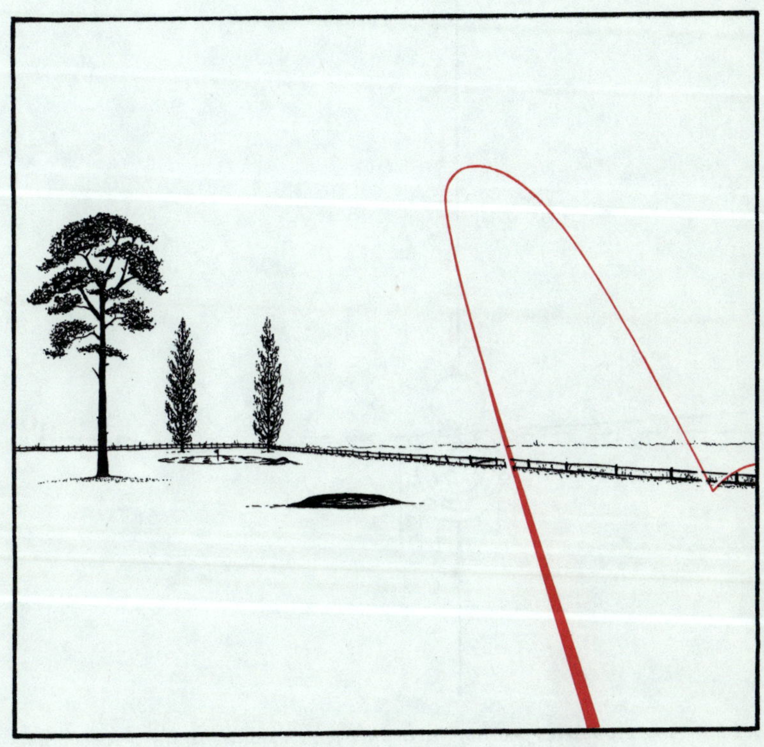

*4:10    A depressingly wild, sliced drive.*

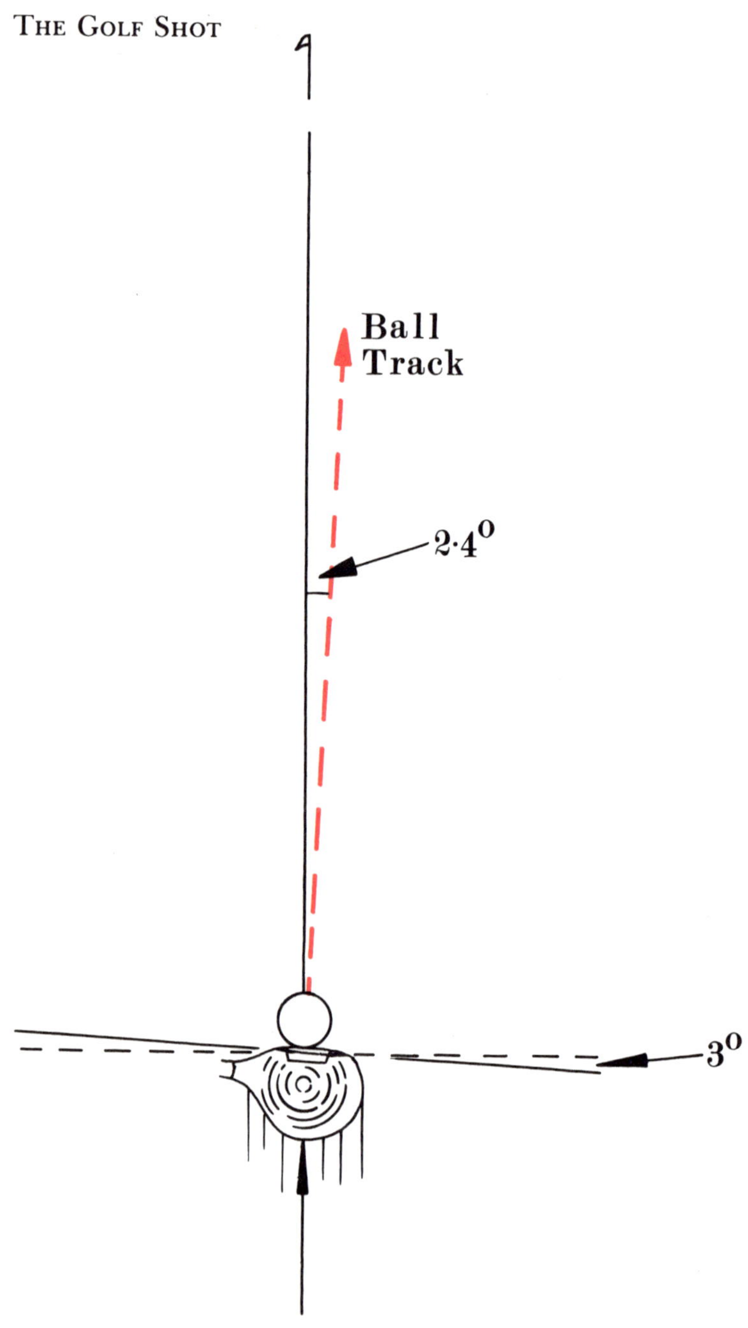


4:11    The club head position at impact which results in the drive shown
in 4:12.

*4:12    A drive with the club face open by 3 degrees at impact.*

opened by 10 degrees in both cases.

The final position of the ball after our sliced 5-iron is less than half the distance off-line than the similarly sliced 1-wood. The shot loses 14 yards in distance compared with the perfectly straight 5-iron. Similar effects are found for hooked shots with the middle irons.

Finally, we shall look at some short iron shots. Diagram 4:15 shows the side view of the perfect 9-iron into a soft

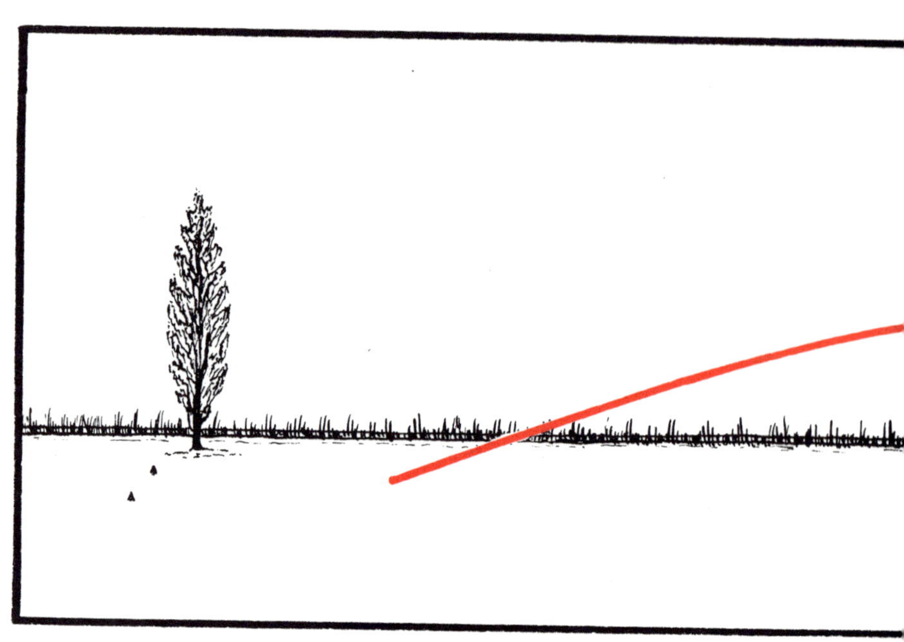

4:13    *A perfect 5-iron recovery shot after a bad drive.*

4:14    *A sliced 5-iron shot with the club face open by 10 degrees at impact. Compare this with the drive shown in 4:4.*

46

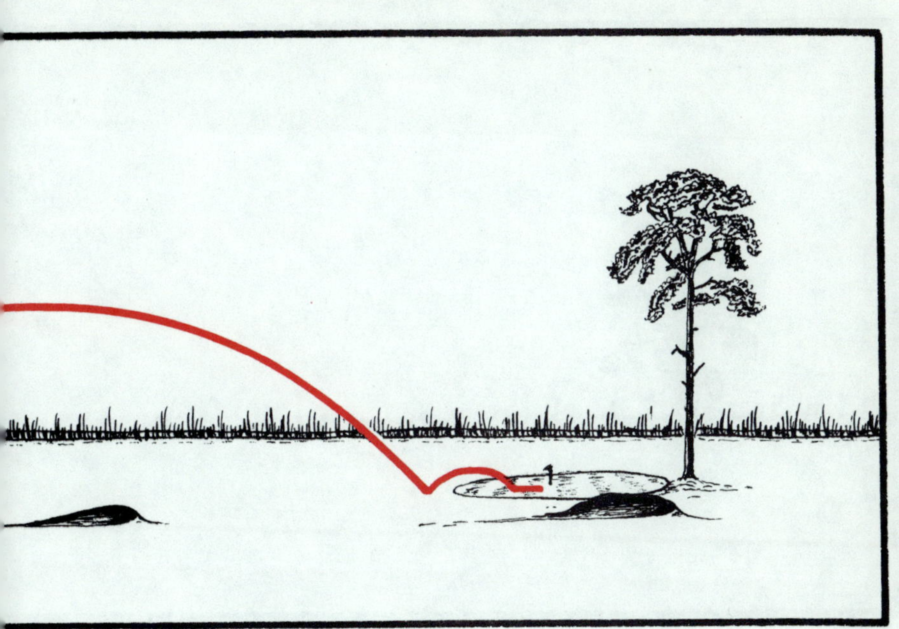

green. The high rate of backspin, about 150 revolutions per second, gives the ball good lift, and again the early part of the shot is nearly straight as lift opposes gravity. The length of the shot is 115 yards.

The pitching wedge has the greatest loft of all the clubs normally used for playing the ball from a fairway lie. This has a face angle of 54 1/2 degrees, and so it is very tolerant as far as swerve is concerned. Even if the club face is considerably out of square, the actual swerve on the ball is small. This is clearly shown in diagram 4:16, which is a wedge shot with the club face opened by 10 degrees again. It can be seen that the main effect on the shot is the fact that the ball starts off to the right of the target. The shot itself is nearly straight. The ball finishes nearly 20 yards to the right of the pin. This indicates that the pitch shot which is off the intended target line is quite possibly, in fact most likely, due

*4:15     A satisfying 9-iron shot to the pin.*

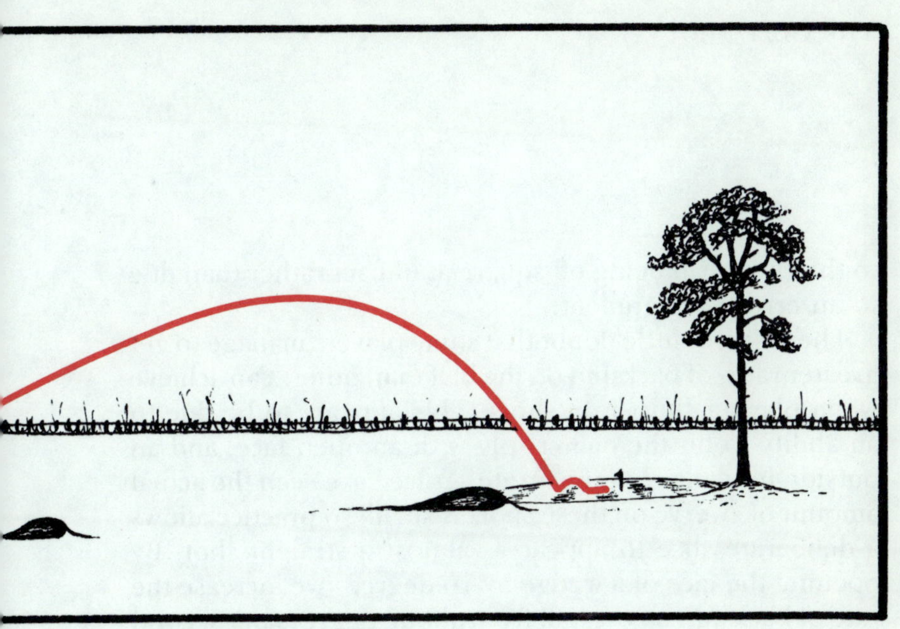

4:16    *A sliced wedge shot with the club face open by 10 degrees at impact. Compare with the shots shown in 4:4 and 4:14.*

to the club head being off square at impact rather than due to an error in alignment.

There seems little doubt that some players manage to get greater rates of backspin on the ball than others can achieve when playing short iron shots. This appears to be due to an ability to hit the ball crisply with an open face, and an outside-in swing to compensate. As we have seen the actual amount of swerve on these shots is small, so practice allows a deliberate slice to appear as almost a straight shot. By opening the face of a wedge by 10 degrees we increase the rate of backspin on the ball from about 174 revs per second to about 187 revs per second. This naturally assists in stopping the ball as it bounces. Careful observation of expert players confirms this opened face approach to pitch shots, and one can often see a divot taken during such a shot fly well off to the left of the line of the shot.

This leads us to consider the implications of deliberately shaped shots with re-aligned swings.

# 5: Shaped Shots

IN THE PREVIOUS CHAPTER we played some shots with the club held incorrectly so that the club face was unintentionally open or closed at impact. The perfectly straight shot is very difficult indeed to achieve, and for this reason really expert golfers usually do not attempt the shot, but rather they aim to deliberately shape the shot in a controlled way. Most professional golfers aim to draw the ball slightly from right to left, while some hit higher, fading shots, moving the ball from left to right. Experience has shown that shots seem to be more reliable and predictable when deliberately curving the ball either one way or the other. In theory, provided that the accuracy of positioning the club head around the "square-on" position is the same as the accuracy of positioning it around the "closed" or "open" positions, then there should be little difference in predictability of shot. However, it does seem that it is easier to achieve a grooved swing in the latter two cases. In addition there is a psychological advantage. The golfer who is fairly sure of being able to draw the ball from right to left and accordingly aims down the right side of the fairway is bound to feel more confident with the whole of the fairway to draw into. This is particularly so if there is trouble on the right. Since a large part of the game of golf is played in the mind before a ball has been struck, this slight extra confidence is bound to be very significant. The same applies to the golfer who can consistently fade the ball and starts it down the left side.

The simplest way to achieve these deliberately curved shots is to re-align the swing by re-aligning the feet in an appropriate way, and then hitting the ball using the normal swing and with the club face either open or closed. The other way is to keep the feet lined up with the target and then to swing with either an "inside-out" or an "outside-in" swing. This is bound to be less predictable and more difficult than always keeping the same swing.

In order to illustrate this type of shot we play a very pronounced draw with a 1-wood. This shows a drive started well out to the right, drawing in and in fact ending about 20 yards to the left of the target. This shot was achieved by lining up at an angle of 33 degrees to the right of the line to the pin and closing the club face by 20 degrees. This

5:1     *A deliberately hooked drive.*

means that at address the club face should still be looking noticeably to the right of the target. This shot would also require a high tee peg and to be hit on the up to achieve the necessary height with such a closed face. This would be difficult to achieve successfully. The shot is shown in diagram 5:1.

We can play a slightly less extreme version of this drive by starting the ball off at an angle of 7 degrees to the right of the line to the flag. This is achieved by re-aligning the swing path, and feet, at an angle of 11 degrees to the right and closing the club face by 5 degrees. Thus, the club face is again looking to the right of the flag. The position at the moment of impact for this shot is shown in diagram 5:2. The resulting rather satisfying shot is shown in diagram 5:3.

Now obviously the golfer does not carry instruments with him to measure angles for his address position. This does not matter, since all we need be concerned with is the general idea of re-aligning the swing and roughly how much we must open or close the face. Every player must determine these positions by practice and experiment. This is certainly a good thing to try at a driving range.

It is, however, easy to give some general guidance on alignment angles. Most players stand at the address position for a drive with the feet about 18 inches apart. If we are attempting to hit a straight shot to the target area, then the feet will be in line with the target or very close to the line. Suppose we wished to turn our line of swing to an angle of 10 degrees to the right of the target line. All we do is move the left foot forward 3 inches and swing normally. For a swing line of 5 degrees to the right, simply move the left foot forward 1 1/2 inches. The important

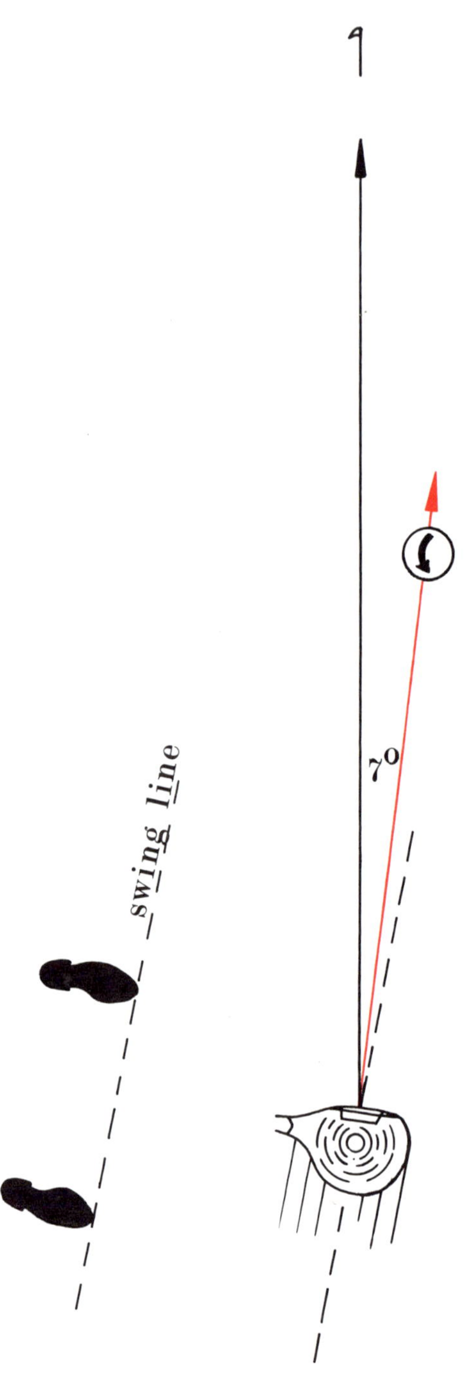


5:2    *Position for the deliberately hooked drive shown in 5:3.*

point here is that the swing should be exactly the same but along a slightly different line.

The same applies for re-aligning left of the target. For a line 10 degrees left of the flag, move the left foot back 3 inches.

As we have seen, having re-aligned our address position, we must either close or open the club face to either draw

5:3    *A drive starting right and drawing in to the pin, using the position shown in 5:2*

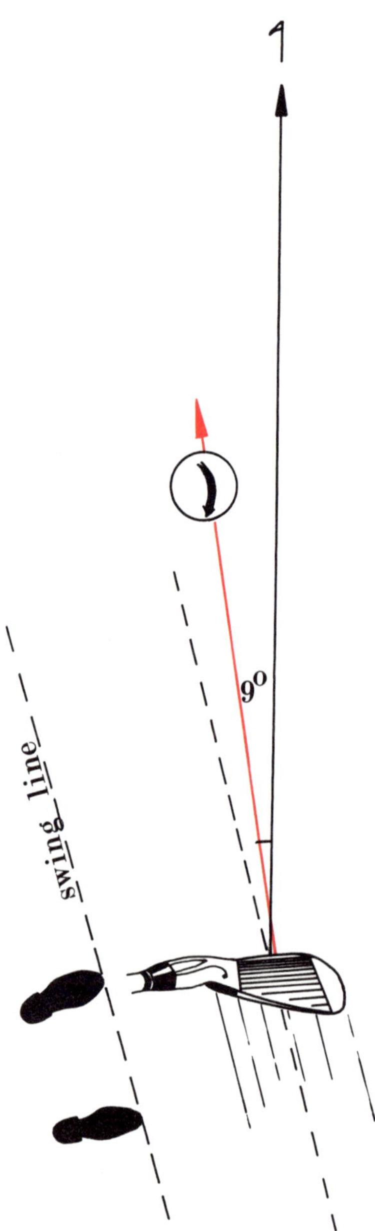



5:4     *Position for the deliberately faded 5-iron shot shown in 5:5.*

or fade the ball to the target. Calculations have shown that for the woods and long irons, the face of the club must look along a line about halfway between the line of address and the line to the target. Thus if we wish to hit a controlled fade to the target, we might move our left foot back about 3 inches, re-aligning ourselves 10 degrees to the left, and the open the club face about 5 degrees. Then we would swing normally through the ball, and we should then fade the ball to near the target area. The same applies for the

*5:5     A faded 5-iron shot using the position shown in 5:4.*

controlled draw, but here we re-align to the right of the target.

The situation is slightly different when we are using the middle irons. As we know, these clubs do not give as much fade or draw as the woods and long irons. Therefore, we must open or close the club face more when using these clubs. Thus for a controlled fade hit with a 5-iron, we should line up left of the target as for the drives, but open

5:6    *A "caddy's eye view" of a deliberately faded 2-iron shot with an unfortunate outcome.*

the club face until it is looking at the target again. The situation at impact for such a shot is shown in diagram 5:4. The resulting shot is shown in diagram 5:5, finishing rather nicely close to the pin.

Again, the same considerations apply when lining up for a deliberate draw. This time the club face is closed until it is looking straight along a line to the flag.

These deliberately shaped shots are very satisfying when they come off, and diagram 5:6. shows a "caddy's-eye-view" of a perfectly executed 2-iron fade into a sand trap.

# 6: Shots through the Wind

THE PRINCIPLES used in calculating the effect of wind on the flight path of a golf shot have been described in Chapter 3. It is important to consider these effects since we rarely play in completely calm conditions. The calculations are made by using the same laws as were used earlier, however the flight thus calculated is relative to the wind which is itself moving relative to the ground. Therefore we must allow for a change in the starting speed and angle to the ground, and also for the distance travelled by the wind during the duration of the shot. Wind tends to be gusty in nature and also to vary with distance above the ground. The presence of trees also affects the wind, which influences the shot. Since it is obviously impossible to take these variations into account in a general sense, we shall simply make a few calculations assuming constant wind speed to illustrate the magnitude of the effect.

For the purposes of demonstrating the effects of wind we shall assume that we are playing in a "fresh breeze" of about 30 feet per second. This is a breeze sufficient to cause small trees to begin to sway and is quite a common condition in which to play golf, especially on seaside courses.

Firstly we shall look at the effect of hitting the ball into a head wind of 30 feet per second. If we hit the ball with the same power as for calm conditions, the starting speed of the ball is the same relative to the ground, but as has been said before, it is *increased* relative to the air. It is greater by an amount equal to the speed of the wind. Therefore, somewhat surprisingly perhaps, the ball travels further relative to the air, but from this we must subtract the distance which the air has moved during the shot. The end result is a shorter shot relative to our own frame of reference, the ground. The increased speed of the ball relative to the air means that the lift force is greater, and this gives a higher shot. This is in spite of the fact that the angle of projection of the ball is slightly smaller entirely because of the head wind. If we play a series of shots into this head wind with a selection of clubs, we can see the effect on shot length and height:

| CLUB | SHOT LENGTH | | SHOT HEIGHT | |
| --- | --- | --- | --- | --- |
| | *Calm* | *Head Wind* | *Calm* | *Head Wind* |
| 1-wood (teed) | 249 1/2 yards | 190 yards | 69 feet | 78 feet |
| 3-wood | 235 1/2 yards | 181 yards | 51 feet | 59 feet |
| 2-iron | 211 yards | 163 yards | 37 feet | 42 feet |
| 3-iron | 203 yards | 150 yards | 61 feet | 70 feet |
| 5-iron | 189 yards | 129 yards | 82 feet | 95 feet |
| 6-iron | 171 yards | 107 yards | 101 feet | 119 feet |
| 7-iron | 154 yards | 93 yards | 99 feet | 118 feet |
| 9-iron | 119 yards | 90 yards | 92 feet | 111 feet |

From this table we can note some interesting confirmation of our ideas of playing into a wind. Firstly, hitting into this fresh breeze we should use about four clubs more to achieve the range needed. Secondly, the lower shots suffer less than the high flying shots, which are really caught by the wind. The middle and short irons suffer additionally due to the steep descent to the ground into the head wind. This almost destroys the bounce and run which we would expect to get on our firm fairway. The 9-iron, which has suffered noticeably less, was hit to a soft green in both cases.

Diagram 6:1 shows two identical 3-iron shots. One is played in still conditions (solid line) and runs right up to the flag. The other is played into the head wind (dashed line) and it falls well short of the green. We should have selected a 3-wood to put the ball on the green in this wind.

We can also see from our tabulated yardages that a short hole which may be within reach with a 5-iron on a still day may require a driver into our head wind.

When we are playing with the same fresh breeze behind the shot the opposite effects are evident. If we hit with the same power as before, the speed of the ball relative to the air is reduced by 30 feet per second compared with calm conditions. Therefore the distance travelled by the ball

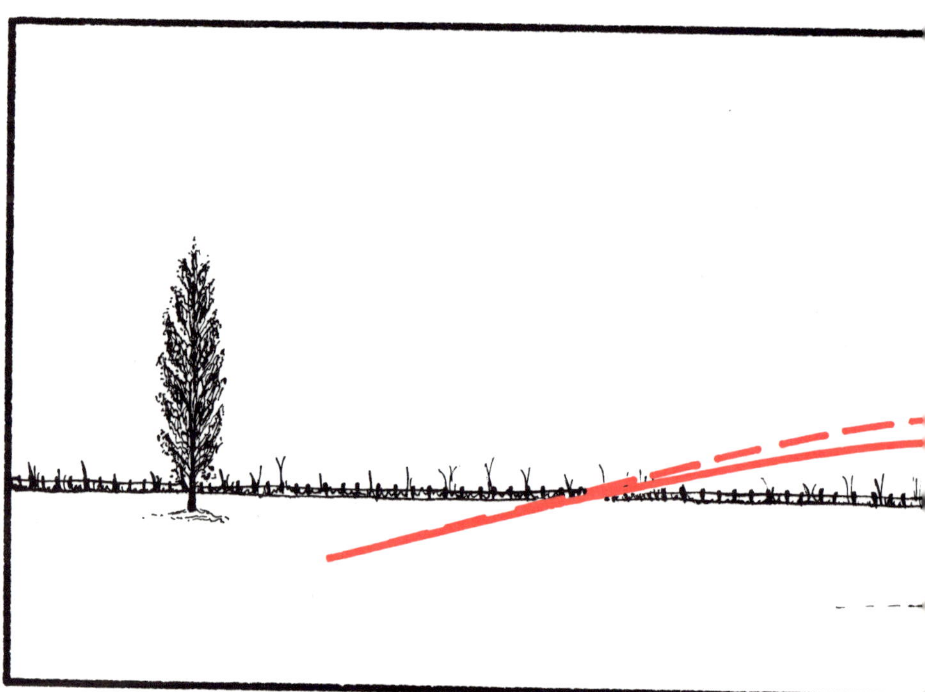

6:1     *Two identically hit 3-iron shots. a) In calm conditions (solid line).*
        *b) Into a "fresh breeze" (dashed line).*

relative to the air is less than in still conditions, but this time we must add the distance travelled by the wind during the shot. The end result is the familiar lengthened shot. The reduced speed through the air reduces the lift force on the ball giving a lower trajectory, in spite of the fact that the angle of projection is slightly greater because of the wind.

We can again play a series of shots through the tail wind and tabulate the yardages:

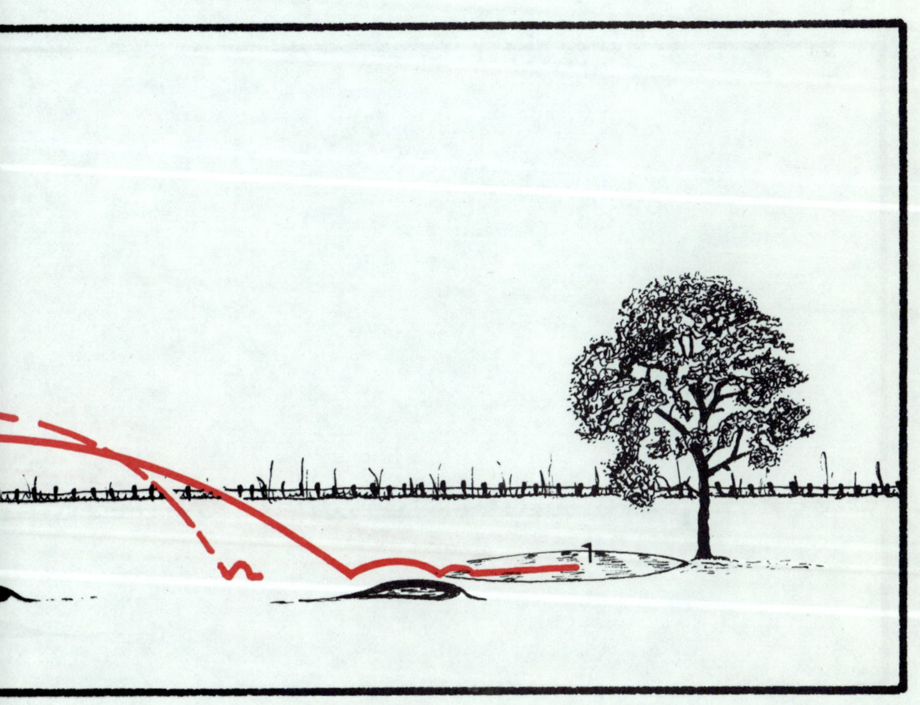

| CLUB | SHOT LENGTH | | SHOT HEIGHT | |
| --- | --- | --- | --- | --- |
| | *Calm* | *Tail Wind* | *Calm* | *Tail Wind* |
| 1-wood (teed) | 249 1/2 yards | 313 yards | 69 feet | 61 feet |
| 3-wood | 235 1/2 yards | 294 yards | 51 feet | 45 feet |
| 2-iron | 211 yards | 262 yards | 37 feet | 32 feet |
| 3-iron | 203 yards | 258 yards | 61 feet | 52 feet |
| 5-iron | 189 yards | 247 yards | 82 feet | 68 feet |
| 6-iron | 171 yards | 227 yards | 101 feet | 80 feet |
| 7-iron | 154 yards | 203 yards | 99 feet | 76 feet |
| 9-iron | 119 yards | 142 yards | 92 feet | 66 feet |

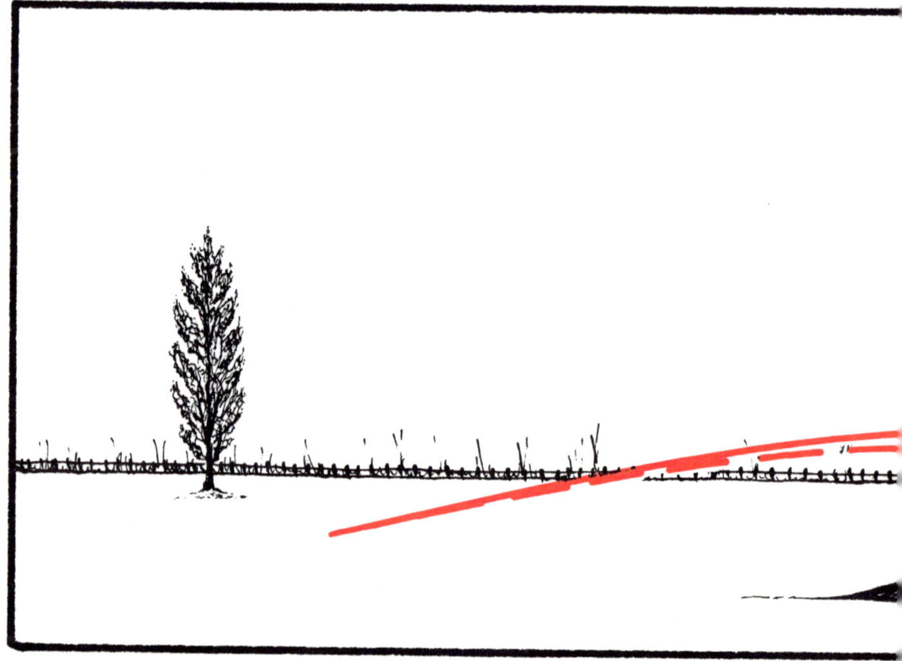

6:2    *Two identically hit 3-iron shots. a) In calm conditions (solid line).*
*b) With a following "fresh breeze" (dashed line).*

These figures illustrate strikingly the way the following wind makes the ball fly noticeably lower due to reduced lift forces. The long irons gain less from the wind since they already give lower shots. It therefore makes sense to use a more lofted club to prolong the flight of the ball and gain maximum advantage. We should use about four clubs less under these conditions, and we can see that a hole which may be a good full drive on a calm day may be reachable with a 4-iron in the tail wind.

A particular hole, say 185 yards long and normally reach-

able with a 5-iron, could vary from being a full drive one day into the wind, to an 8-iron the next day if the wind veered round to the opposite direction. This is typical of play on exposed seaside courses.

Diagram 6:2 shows two identical 3-iron shots. One is played in calm conditions (solid line) and is successful, while the other is in the fresh tail wind (dashed line) and goes way over the back of the green.

Crosswinds provide some interesting decisions regarding the type of shot to be played. There are two main possibilities when playing through a stiff cross breeze. Firstly, we can use the wind and, for example, aim left of the target in a left to right wind and allow the wind to help the ball back into the target zone. Secondly, we can attempt to hit an appropriately drawn shot in the wind, relying on the draw to counteract the effect of the wind. The first of these is likely to be more reliable since it does not depend on obtaining the correct amount of swerve, only requiring the correct line of swing to be chosen. Furthermore the ball will travel slightly further if we allow the wind to help the flight. For these reasons we shall restrict ourselves to illustrating the effects of crosswinds on shots which would normally be perfectly straight, and to indicating the amount of adjustment of line which is necessary for our fresh cross breeze of 30 feet per second.

Diagram 6:3 shows a drive through a left to right breeze. This shot would have been perfectly straight under still conditions, and would have finished by the flag. The actual shot flies very slightly higher than normal, and finishes no less than 50 yards to the right if it has enough room to run on. This means that we should have lined up an equivalent amount left of the flag to give the shot room to fade back onto the fairway.

Diagram 6:4 shows the equivalent shot in a right to left wind with no allowance made.

Lower flying shots will tend to suffer less in crosswinds, and this will obviously influence our choice of club.

6:3    *A drive hit in a fresh left to right cross wind. In calm conditions the ball would have finished near the pin.*

6:4    *A drive hit in a fresh right to left cross wind. In calm conditions the ball would have finished near the pin.*

# 7: Playing from Elevated Tees

THE GOLF SHOT from an elevated tee or fairway is a deceptive one, and it is easy to misjudge the club required. The first part of the shot is obviously unaffected by the lowered landing area, but the ultimate length of the shot is increased since the arc of the shot is extended. The ball spends slightly longer in the air before landing, and so the effects of any wind will be slightly increased. We can demonstrate the effects of playing a series of shots to lowered greens using our computer 'player'. For tee elevations of 10 feet, 20 feet and 30 feet the shot lengths are as follows:

| Club | Level | 10 feet | 20 feet | 30 feet |
| --- | --- | --- | --- | --- |
| 1-wood | 250 | 254 | 258 | 262 |
| 3-wood | 236 | 238 | 243 | 247 |
| 2-iron | 211 | 212 | 214 | 219 |
| 3-iron | 203 | 208 | 212 | 216 |
| 5-iron | 189 | 193 | 197 | 200 |
| 6-iron | 171 | 175 | 178 | 181 |
| 7-iron | 154 | 157 | 161 | 164 |
| 9-iron | 119 | 121 | 124 | 130 |

The effects can be seen to be similar on all shots, an addition of around 10 yards when shooting from an elevation of 30 feet to a *level* landing area. We are most interested in this sort of effect when playing par 3 holes using middle irons from elevated tees. The calculations show that we should use about one club less when playing such a hole from an elevated tee compared with the same distance on level ground.

Diagram 7:1 shows the extended arc in the case of a drive from a tee elevated by 30 feet. Naturally, some tees are more elevated than others. There have been various holes designed in which the green was well down below the tee, perhaps in a quarry. In playing this type of hole, it is the difficulty in believing that the ball still has to be hit and not just popped over the edge which provides the challenge. One of the more extreme versions of this type of hole was the ninth at Lincoln Park, San Francisco, on the cliffs just outside the Golden Gate. This was in the days when it

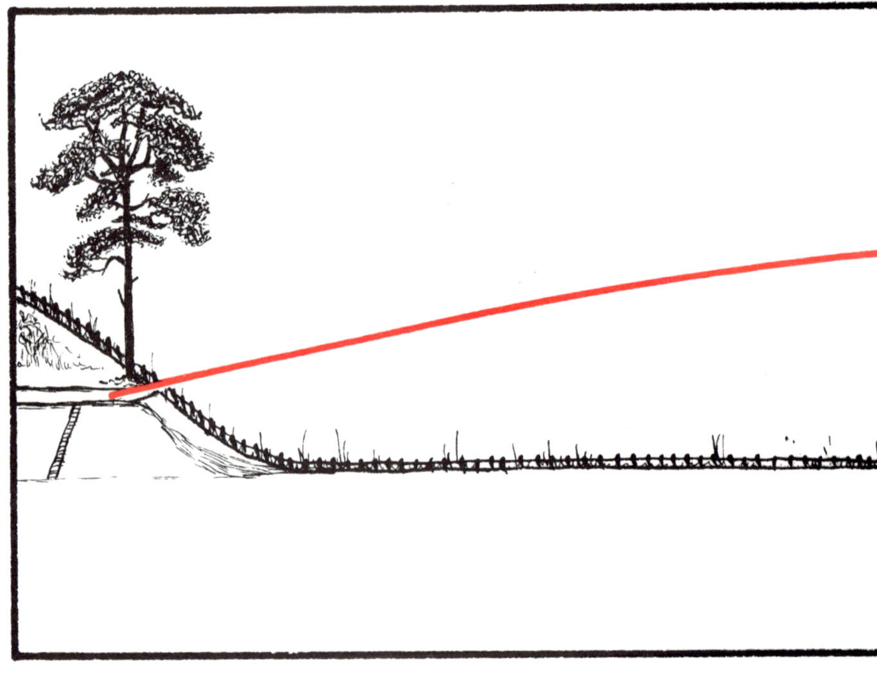

7:1　　*The extended arc of a drive hit from a tee elevated by 30 ft. The drive is about 12 yards longer than it would have been from a tee on a level with the green.*

was a nine hole course, and the ninth hole is reputed to have been a straight drop of 500 feet to a green at the ocean's edge, directly below the eighth green! Playing this hole late on a summer afternoon, with the fog rolling in from the ocean and reducing the visibility to a few yards, must have given something of an advantage to the player with local knowledge.

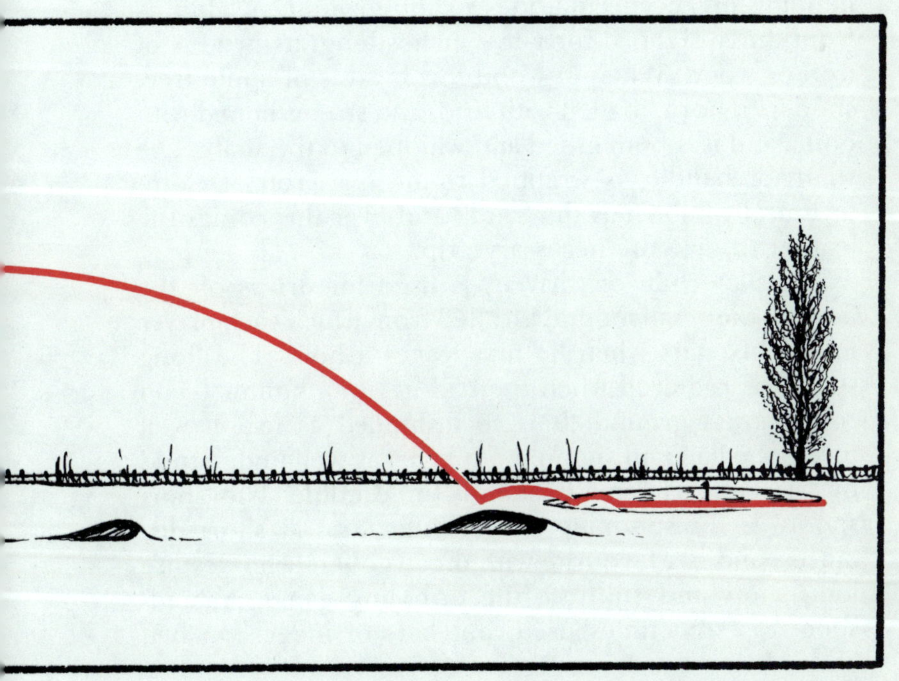

# 8: Club and Ball

Modern golf equipment reflects the technological advances which have been made during this century. Clubs have become much more precise; standardised, but with a wide range of types available. There are variations available in shaft stiffness, length of shaft, lie, grip etc. It is a far cry from the individual clubs of former times. The following description of a set of golf clubs appeared in *Outdoor Games and Recreations,* published in 1892:

> A set of clubs numbers about a dozen, the varieties depending on the peculiarities of the ground. A 'club' is from thirty-eight to forty-five inches long; its head is of iron or wood. When of wood this head is of apple tree, shod with horn, loaded with lead, and strengthened with bone, and it is both glued and whipped to the shaft. The shaft, or handle, is wrapped round by a roll of cloth, technically known as the 'rind', and over this comes the leather to give the necessary grip.
>
> The play-club, or 'driver', is used for drives off the 'tee', as the small mound is called from which each player makes his start when he first leaves a hole. The 'long spoon' is required when the ball lies in a hollow or on rough grass ground. It is so fashioned as to get well under the ball and spoon it out in a way well understood by cricketers as being eminently undesirable. The 'short spoon' is for spooning out of difficulties at short distances, and is a favourite with those golfers who despise long shots and cultivate the dribbling game. A 'mid-spoon' is sometimes used, but lads of indecision had better leave it at home.
>
> Shorter than the short spoon is the most difficult of all tools, the 'baffing spoon', so moulded as to give a still higher and shorter curve. To 'baff' at golf is to hit the

ground as well as the ball, and with the baffer the ball is hit well under so as to 'loft' and fall near the hole. Besides the driver and four spoons, there are four irons and a pair of putters.

The 'driving putter'—the word rhymes to butter—is short and stiff in the shank and large and heavy in the head; it hits almost along the ground, and is a most valuable club on smooth greens. The 'putter' itself is square faced, and is used for putting the ball, and the way in which the small white globe curves off the iron handled putter for thirty yards and more clean into the tiny cylindrical hole, is perhaps the most startling thing in the golfing novitiate. The learner stands a very poor chance when matched against an adroit performer with this most useful tool.

The sandy banks, furze-bushes, cart ruts, gravel walks, macadamised roads, and other obstacles round the course, are known as hazards, and to get out of some of these the 'sand iron' has to be brought into play. Its head has a centre hollow, while that of its cousin, the 'cleek', is straight. For cart ruts and similar depressions the niblick is used. It is a small sand iron with a hollow about two inches across. The fourth iron is the 'putting cleek', which is simply the missing link between the cleek and the niblick, or 'track iron', as it is not infrequently called.

This description shows the way that our approach to the game has changed in recent times. The old game involved much more maneuvering of the ball with a limited number of weapons, rather than the modern clinical approach of careful choice of club for a required distance. It is sad that all the marvellous traditional names for the various clubs have been all but lost.

It is interesting that the same 1892 publication provides the following coaching on how to hold and swing the club:

> . . . the golf club is held by the best players exactly as a girl holds a cricket bat! The left hand comes near the top, with the knuckles on the driving side, the right hand lightly touching the left as it grasps the leather below, while the wrists are allowed full play, so as to give the club an easy swing, increasing gradually in strength as the ball is reached. A golf club, when properly swung, describes a three-quarter circle. It is not easy to hit the ball fair and true; it is not necessary to hit it violently. In swiping, the left foot should be placed opposite to the ball, with a 'stance', or distance from it of thirty inches, and the feet should be about eighteen inches apart. If the player stands too near the ball he will 'heel' it off; if he stands too far from it he will 'hook' it round. To hit straight, his position must be accurately judged, and he must keep his eye on the ball.

This provides quite a vivid contrast with the thousands of words and illustrations which have appeared in modern books on golf technique.

There are a couple of interesting points which have emerged as a result of relatively recent studies of the characteristics of golf clubs. The first concerns the effect of the weight of the club head on the effectiveness of the club. It can be shown theoretically that there is an optimum, or 'ideal', value for the weight of the club head. This comes about because the velocity of the ball leaving a club head travelling at a given speed increases as the club head weight increases. However, it is apparent that there is some reduction in the efficiency of energy transfer with increasing club head weight, and furthermore a player will be unable to swing very heavy clubs as fast as lighter ones. Since there are opposing effects, there will be an optimum weight for the club head when we get the maximum advantage without too much of the disadvantage. Calculations show that this ideal weight is about 200 grams, and this agrees very well with the accepted practice which has been arrived at, based on years of trial and error. The optimum weight appears to be the same for strong and weak players.

The other point of interest concerns the practice of grooving the club face. The Rules of Golf are quite specific on this point. For example: *When the depressed area (on the club face) is in the form of grooves, each groove may not be wider than 0.035 inches (approximately one thirty-second of an inch) (0.9 mm), the angle between the flat surface of the club face and the side of the groove may not be less than 135 degrees. Except as provided elsewhere, the distance between grooves may not be less than three times the width of the groove.*

However, detailed studies on the events which occur during the split second that the club and ball are in contact seem to show that the roughness of the face is unlikely to have any influence on the amount of backspin given to the ball. This is because, as the club hits the ball, the ball starts to slide up the face and then begins to roll up it. The duration of the sliding phase is very short indeed and, although this duration may be slightly longer in the case of a smooth face, nevertheless there is always time for the rolling to become established. It is this rolling which gives the ball its backspin. Therefore the theory indicates that the amount of backspin given to the ball should be the same for smooth-faced clubs as for clubs with carefully grooved faces. This is a somewhat surprising prediction, but it has been confirmed as being correct by experimental observations in which golf balls were hit with identical clubs except that some had smooth faces while the others had conventionally grooved faces. The resulting spin, length of carry and run on the ball were identical. These experiments were carried out with 5-irons, 7-irons and 9-irons. So it seems that the careful preparation of the club face is a waste of time, and only adds to the cost of clubs. However, we are so used to thinking that the roughened face assists the iron shots that a manufacturer who produced smooth faced clubs would undoubtedly have some difficulty with sales.

There have been some interesting variations in clubs produced over the years, like the club with the adjustable face angle, the toothed 'water-mashie' and the mallet-type putters. It is also not unknown for an entire set of modern clubs to be woods, right up to a 9-wood and putter.

The other piece of equipment which is absolutely essential is the ball. The golf ball has had an interesting history. Up to the middle of the nineteenth century the ball consisted of feathers stuffed into a leather cover; the 'feathery'. The feathers were soft boiled and the number of feathers was the amount which would fill a 'lum hat', a hat popular at the time.

In 1848 the gutta-percha ball, the 'gutty', was invented, and this must have revolutionized the game. Originally the gutty ball was smooth, but it rapidly became obvious that as soon as the ball had been hit a number of times and the surface had become dented, it flew considerably further. It was logical therefore to produce balls with a hammered surface, thus originating the present day dimples. Fortunately we have some information on the physical characteristics of the gutty, as well as some reports on the way it performed. In those days it was common to have a ball remade when it became damaged.

Around 1902 the rubber-cored ball was developed, and in 1920 the Royal and Ancient standardized the size of the ball at not less than 1.62 inches diameter, the maximum weight being 1.62 ounces. In the United States the ball with a minimum diameter of 1.68 inches was made official in 1943.

Recently a different type of ball has appeared, this being made from a solid polymeric material. There is no central core, the ball simply being a sphere of plastic. One of the claimed advantages of this type of ball is that it should be less easily damaged by mis-hits. It is, however, possible for the ball to shatter at the instant that the club hits it, and this is a somewhat disconcerting experience.

Using information which is available on some early types of ball, we can play some drives with a variety of old-time balls so that we can see how the game has gradually changed. There appears to have been a good deal of variation in the size and weight of the gutty ball. One type appears to have had a weight of only 1.13 ounces and a diameter of about 1.6 inches. It also had a noticeably lower value of the 'coefficient of restitution', or 'bounciness', and this means that the ball started with a lower speed for a given club head speed. All these characteristics of the ball conspired to shorten the drive considerably. We will play a drive with this ball and see what happens. If we use the same club head speed as for our perfect drive described in chapter 4, which gave a drive of 249 1/2 yards with a modern ball, we achieve a total shot length of 195 yards. The shot flies slightly lower, reaching a maximum height of 64 feet compared with 69 feet for the modern ball. The 'carry' of this full-out drive is only 163 yards. The reduction in drive length compared with the modern ball shows the way that a 350-yard hole would have changed its character.

With the modern ball, such a hole is a drive and a 9-iron for a good player. With the gutty which we have just used for a drive, the hole would require a drive and a 3-iron, or, for the old-timers, a drive and a mid-mashie. This all means that a hole which is a simple par-4 with the modern ball would have been almost a par-5 with our old gutty.

The tendency over a period of many years has been for golf courses to lengthen by pushing tees further and further back. This is not necessarily a good thing, giving as it does longer walks between green and tee and changing the character of the holes. Our shot with the gutty illustrates why this has happened. In 1892 the average length of the holes on the Old Course at St. Andrews was given as about 350 yards, making a total length of 6300 yards. The length of the Old Course today is 6581 yards, showing that it has not lengthened noticeably. However, the same source mentions that the 'average length of a golf round is three miles', or 5280 yards, and this is considerably shorter than most modern courses. Also in 1892, at St. Andrews: 'it takes the best players five strokes to get from one to the other' (tee to hole).

One consolation for the player using our old gutty was that it would float in water, giving the opportunity for some fancy shots out of water hazards. Such a shot, played from a rowing boat, formed a part of one of the golf stories by P.G.Wodehouse. Whether a 'toothed water-mashie' was selected is not known.

Another make of gutty ball was reported by Professor Tait in 1890 as having a diameter of 1.75 inches and a weight of 1.62 ounces. A full drive with this ball would give a length of 219 yards, the carry being 177 yards. This confirms the remark made by Tait in 1893 that "180 yards is a really fine carry", and it illustrates the fact that the change in the modern game has come about almost entirely because of improvements in ball design, since our shot with a modern club gave a shot similar to that reported at a time when old-fashioned clubs were in use.

After the turn of the century, with the rubber-cored ball well established, wide variations still existed. Discussion went on for years on the merits of defining a standard ball. In 1929 a poem by Sir Owen Seaman appeared in *Punch* magazine entitled 'The Standard Golf Ball', the first verse of which read as follows:

> *I do not want a standard ball,*
> *So many to the pound,*
> *Whether they stuff its inner void*
> *With rubber, wool or celluloid,*
> *I hardly seem to care at all*
> *So long as it is round.*

Before 1932 in the U.S. one brand of ball had a diameter of 1.68 inches and a weight of 1.55 ounces. If we drive this ball in the same way as before we achieve a drive of 236 yards. Another early type was called the 'Why Not', and was a heavier ball. It had a weight of 1.68 ounces and a diameter of 1.62 inches. Even though this ball had a lower coefficient of restitution than the modern high compression ball, a drive with this ball would be 247 yards. This is virtually the same as the modern ball.

From 1943 in the U.S. the official ball has conformed to the present rules. An early version of this ball, again with a lower compression, gives a drive of 239 yards. All these shots described are hit with identical force.

Let us look now at the performance of the modern high compression ball. As we saw earlier, it has been apparent for many years that the presence of a roughened surface of some kind is very important to the flight of the ball. In order to demonstrate the importance, we will play a drive with a modern ball, but one with a perfectly smooth surface and no dimples. A curious effect here is that the backspin given to the ball is a distinct disadvantage. The lift forces, which are so important in drives with the dimpled ball, completely disappear, and in fact become negative. In other words the backspin actually pulls the ball rapidly downwards. The result is that our full-out drive achieves the magnificant carry of 70 yards. This surprising result has been confirmed many times with golf driving machines, and using this type of ball would make the game a very different proposition.

Oddly enough, at higher rates of backspin above about 100 revolutions per second, the lift force on a smooth ball again pulls upwards. Thus a smooth ball played with a middle to short iron would again obtain lift. However this lift would never be as great as is experienced by a dimpled ball, and furthermore the drag of the air on the smooth ball would be similar to that on a dimpled ball at these rates of backspin. There would therefore still be a considerable disadvantage in using a smooth ball.

The modern ball has 333 dimples, each with a depth of 0.0135 inches. In the course of development, there have been a number of different types of surface. Some of the gutties had simple straight grooves around the ball, while others had star-shaped indentations. 'Mesh Balls' were common some years ago, the surface being a lattice pattern with square shaped depressions. There was also the 'Bramble' which had protruding pimples all over the surface. Tests have shown that these latter two types perform in an identical way to the dimpled ball.

Some tests were made on a ball with conventionally

shaped dimples, but of reduced depth. The lift forces experienced by this type were intermediate between the normal ball and the smooth type, but nearer to the normal ball.

The newer 'solid type' ball tends to have lower rates of backspin than the rubber-cored ball, and so the dimples could be made slightly deeper to compensate. However, measurements on a selection of brands failed to reveal any significant difference in depth. The solid types do give lower trajectories due to the smaller lift forces.

In the U.K. the official ball is slightly smaller than the U.S. ball, 1.62 inches compared with 1.68 inches. This means that it is illegal in the U.S. The smaller diameter gives a longer drive, and if we now play a drive with this ball we get a total shot of 262 yards compared with 249 1/2 yards with the U.S. ball.

There are limitations imposed on the coefficient of restitution for a golf ball. This coefficient is about 0.7 for the modern high compression ball. Values of about 0.6 were typical for the gutty, and 0.64 for the early rubber-cored ball. This means that these earlier types left the club head with a lower speed when hit with the same force. The rule governing the coefficient of restitution is as follows: *The velocity of the ball shall not be greater than 250 feet (76.2 m) per second when measured on apparatus approved by the Royal and Ancient Golf Club of St Andrews: a maximum tolerance of 2% will be allowed. The temperature of the ball when so tested shall be 75 degrees Fahrenheit (24 degrees Centigrade).* The apparatus hits the ball in a similar way to a drive, and so measures the coefficient of restitution under playing conditions. The reason that the temperature is specified for the test is that the value of the coefficient of restitution varies with temperature. As the ball gets colder, the coefficient gets smaller, so the speed of the ball off the club face gets slower. This is the main reason that shots do not fly as far under winter conditions. We can show this effect by playing our standard drive in frosty conditions. The coefficient is about 0.62 for a ball which would have a value of 0.7 at 68°F, a normal ball. Assuming the bounce and run conditions are the same, the drive ends up at 235 yards, so we have lost about 15 yards compared with summer conditions. This fact has resulted in some golfers trying to keep the ball warm during winter play. There are warmers on the market to achieve just this. One thing to remember here is that rubber has a low value of a property called the "thermal diffusivity", which means that it is difficult for the heat to make its way into the interior of the ball, as it must to have any effect. It is not enough for just the surface of the ball to be warm. Calculations have shown that a matter of an hour or more must pass before the interior of the ball is warm, having warmed the surface. This can work to our advantage, however, since heat in the ball also has trouble getting out. It therefore takes a considerable time for a thoroughly warm ball to cool down in play. Therefore if we make sure the ball is warmed before winter play, it will retain its improved performance for a considerable time.

The velocity of the ball off the club face comes as we saw in Chapter 3, from the fact that the ball is flattened to a considerable extent at the instant of impact, and then regains its spherical shape and leaves the club face behind. There is some loss of energy during this process, and the less the amount of flattening the less the energy loss. So the 'high compression' ball flattens less than the 'low compression' ball, and hence retains more energy and leaves with a higher speed. The amount of flattening experienced by the ball is quite surprising, and is shown in diagram 8:1. The dashed area represents the flattened area on the face of a 1-wood. The area of contact is over half the maximum cross sectional area of the undeformed ball. This is quite easy to demonstrate by using carbon paper between the club face and the ball.

The diameter of the flattened area is about 1 1/4 inches. For a correctly hit shot this should be entirely within the face of the club, otherwise some unwelcome deflection will be produced by the ball squashing over the edge of the

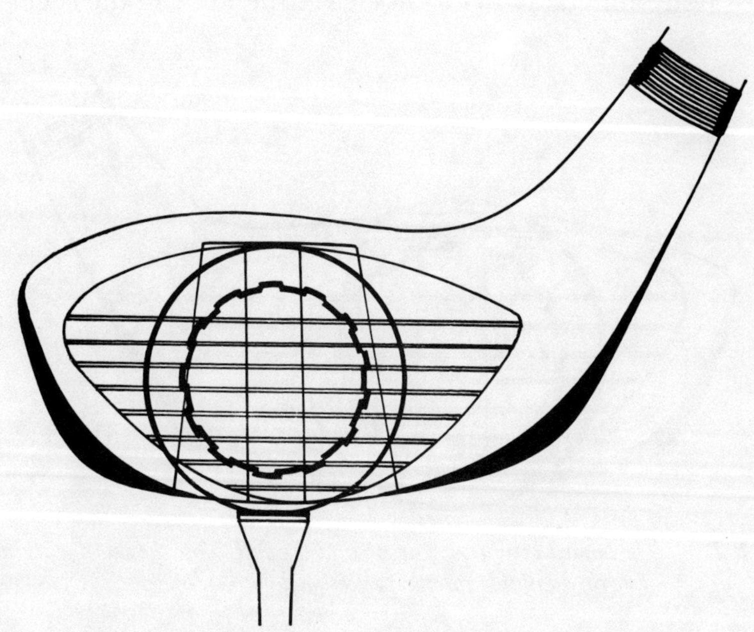

8:1      *The impact between a 1-wood and the ball. The dashed circle shows the extent of the flattened area on the side of the ball.*

face. The depth of a 1-wood might typically be about 1 1/2 inches, and that of a 3-wood might itself be only about 1 1/4 inches. Diagram 8:2 shows the ball at impact on the face of a 3-wood, and once again we see the small margin of error which is available to the golfer. This again emphasises the extraordinary accuracy with which the club head is delivered to the ball in the course of a perfect shot. 'Topped' and 'skied' shots occur when the club head is either too high or too low at impact, causing the ball to squash itself partly around either the bottom or top edge of the face. Diagram 8:3 shows a side view of the extent of flattening.

Many golfers try to get an idea of the value of the coeffi-

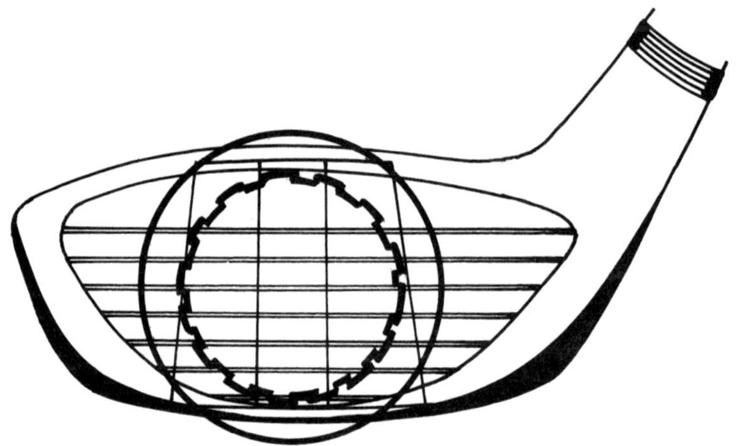

8:2     *The impact between a 3-wood and the ball. Note the small margin of error available for the perfect shot.*

cient of restitution of a golf ball by bouncing it on a cement floor. If we drop a ball from a known height and measure the height of the rebound, then the ratio: height of bounce/height of drop is equal to the coefficient squared. For example, if a ball is dropped from 36 inches and rebounds to a height of 22 inches, the ratio of the rebound to the drop is 0.61, and the square root of this is 0.78. This seems to indicate a value of the coefficient of restitution of 0.78. However the ball was travelling very slowly during this test,

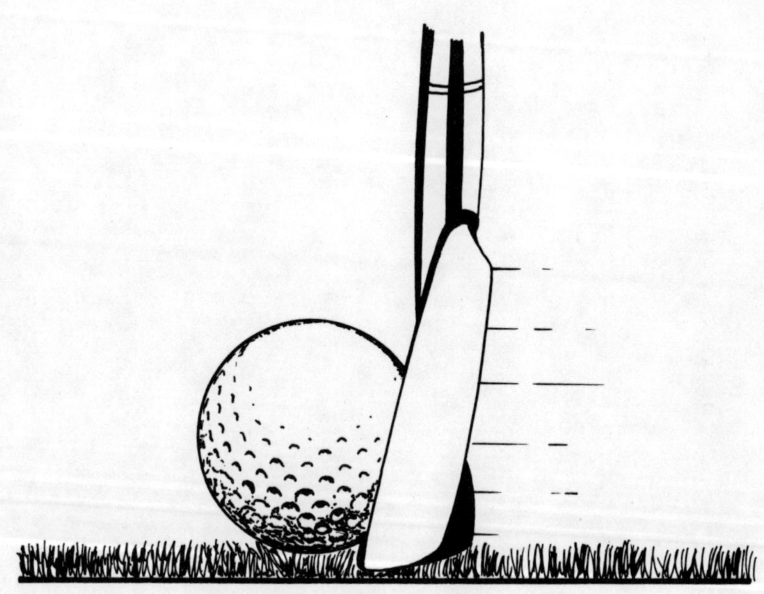

8:3     *The extent of flattening of the ball at impact.*

and this bears little relationship to the performance of the ball when hit by a driver in actual play. The performance depends on the speed of impact, and this is why the rule governing the ball contains a measurement at high impact speed.

Perhaps the strangest golf ball of all is one recently developed, in the shape of a cube, for playing golf on the decks of ships at sea. On some days it seems that playing with such a ball on dry land would make little difference.

# 9: Putting

Putting the ball into the hole is a very important part of golf, some might say that it has too great an importance compared with other parts of the game. The motion of the ball across the putting surface is heavily dependent on the condition of the grass, the grain and the slopes in the green. It is therefore difficult to analyse the process in detail because of the variety of situations which arise. However we can make a few interesting calculations which illustrate the margin of error which is available to us as we approach a putt.

Observations made on putts across a flat green have shown that a starting velocity of about 13 feet per second is necessary to achieve a 33 foot putt. We can use this fact to calculate the extent of rolling friction which slows the ball as it rolls across a typical putting surface. Actually, the very early part of any putt consists of the ball sliding across the grass, but it quickly starts to roll. We shall only consider the rolling part of the putt.

The object of the putt, of course, is to get the ball to drop into the 4 1/4 inch diameter hole. If the ball arrives at the hole with too great a speed it will jump right over the hole. We can quite easily calculate the fastest speed at which we can be sure of the ball dropping into the hole. This is done by considering what happens to the ball as it becomes airborne over the front lip of the hole. As soon as it becomes airborne it is acted on by gravity, and it starts to curve downwards. We must now make a decision about how it must strike the back of the hole to be sure of success. The most reasonable assumption here is probably that the ball must strike the back of the hole with its centre at least down to ground level. If the ball is any higher as it hits the back there is a possibility of it jumping over, depending on the care with which the hole has been cut. Our limiting condition is shown in diagram 9:1. Having decided on this, it is possible to establish that the maximum speed the ball can have at the front lip of the hole is 4.3 feet per second. It is also obvious that the minimum speed the ball must have is 0 feet per second if it is to just crawl into the hole. Therefore for any putt it appears that we must hit the ball so that it has a final speed at the hole in the range 0 to 4.3 feet per second. This is the range between a 'dribbler' and a 'gobbler'. Now we can calculate, for any length of putt, the range of starting speed which we have available for a successful putt.

For example, we find that for a 10 foot putt over a perfectly flat green, the ball must have a starting speed of 7.2 feet per second if it is just to reach the hole; and it must have a starting speed of 8.4 feet per second if it is to reach the hole at 4.3 feet per second, our maximum allowable speed. Therefore we must strike the ball in such a way as to give it a starting speed in the range 7.2 to 8.4 feet per second. If we can manage this, and if we have got the line correct, the putt will drop. This means that we have an allowable error in starting speed of 17% for our 10 foot putt. We can do the same calculation for other lengths of putt, and diagram 9:2 shows the way that the percentage of available error changes with the length of putt. It is clearly shown in this diagram that the judgement of correct speed gets rapidly more difficult as the putt gets longer. For short putts we have a large margin of error available, and consequently it is not difficult to get within it. However this margin gets rapidly less for longer putts, and this is why we all find it difficult to sink long putts even if we get the line correct. The more skilful the golfer, the smaller will his error in speed be, and the more of those long putts will he sink. The expert golfer can probably expect to get the speed correct most of the time for, say, 20 foot putts, indicating an error of less than 10% in hitting the ball.

Obviously, many putts are missed, not because the speed of the ball is wrong, but because the ball is hit along the wrong line. In this context, it is interesting to note that, if the ball passes the side of the hole at our maximum drop-

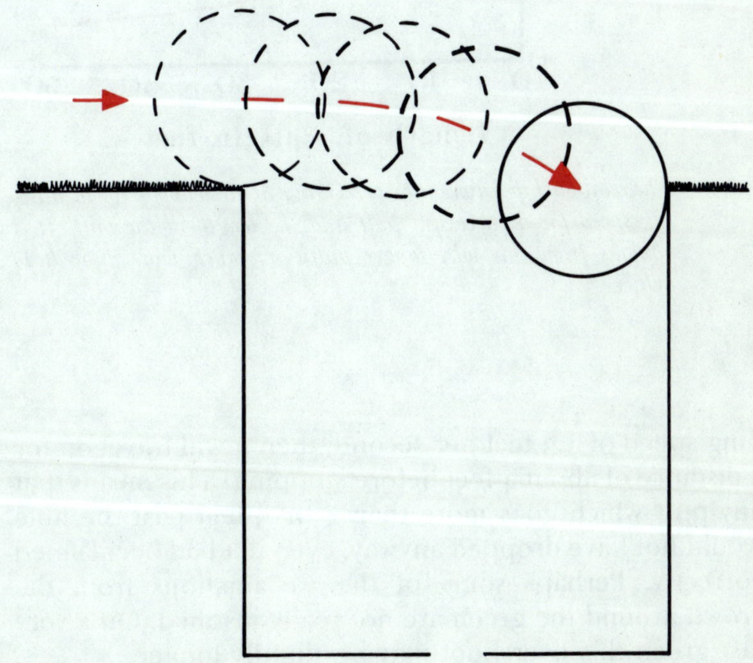

9:1    *The limiting condition for the fastest possible successful putt.*

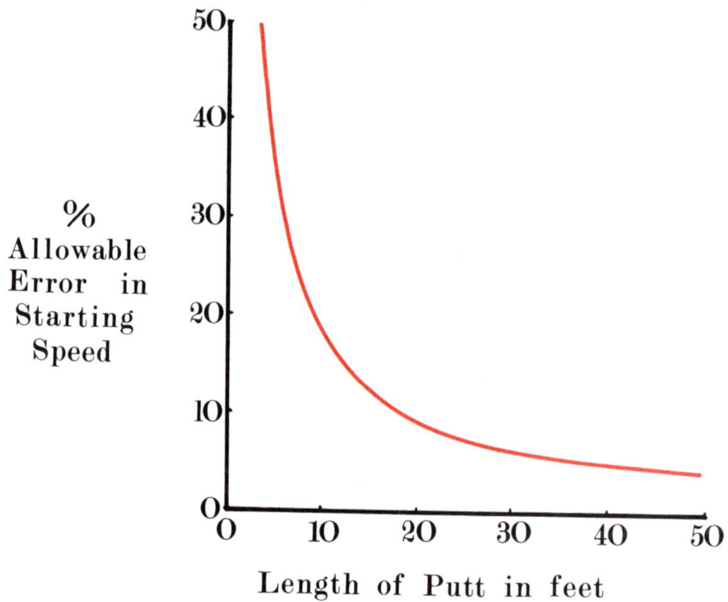

9:2    *The relationship between the percentage of allowable error in start-ing speed for a successful putt and the length of the putt. It is obvious from this why longer putts are much more difficult to achieve.*

ping speed of 4.3 feet per second, then it will travel on for a distance of about 4 feet before stopping. This means that any putt which goes more than 4 or 5 feet past the hole would not have dropped anyway, even if it had been aimed correctly. Perhaps some of the exclamations from the crowd around the green are not really justified. On a very fast green this overshoot may be slightly longer.

In the cases of uphill putts and downhill putts the allowable range of starting speeds will be slightly different. Theoretically the uphill putt is slightly easier since gravity slows the ball as well as pulling it down while it goes into the hole. However on the sort of gradients encountered on putting greens this is a small effect.

Probably of greater importance in the cases of long uphill putts and long downhill putts is the desire to leave the ball near enough to the hole to make the next putt a formality. On a downhill putt, if we hit the ball so that it arrives at the hole with the maximum allowable speed of 4.3 feet per second, and if we have not judged the line correctly, the ball would go a long way past. For example, putting down a 3 degree slope, a gradient of 1 in 20, the 4 foot overshoot which we had on a level green would become 10 feet. This would be a very difficult second putt.

Suppose we want to be sure of leaving the ball within 2 feet of the hole. For a putt of 20 feet up a 3 degree slope our range of starting speeds is 12.4 feet per second to leave the ball 2 feet short, to 13.7 feet per second to leave the ball 2 feet past. Thus the range of starting speeds available to us is 1.3 feet per second. Now, for the same length of putt *down* the same slope, the corresponding speeds are 5.7 feet per second and 6.3 feet per second, a range of 0.6 feet per second. This shows why the 'slider', or downhill putt is much more demanding than the same putt uphill.

Diagram 9:3 shows the results if we do the same calculations for other lengths of putt. Again we see how the longer putts are more difficult, and also the noticeable difference in difficulty between uphill putts and downhill putts. Some of the trouble experienced with downhill putts is probably associated with the difficulty in believing how slowly the ball must be struck. The rolling friction which has been used here indicates that, down a slope of 4.6 degrees, a gradient of 1 in 12, the ball would continue rolling indefinitely until it reached flatter territory.

We often find ourselves faced with a putt along the side of a slope, and we have to allow a 'borrow' in order to align the putt correctly. The amount of borrow for a particular putt depends on the steepness of the slope, the length of the putt and also on the speed of putt which we choose to hit. For example, suppose we are confronted with a 10 foot

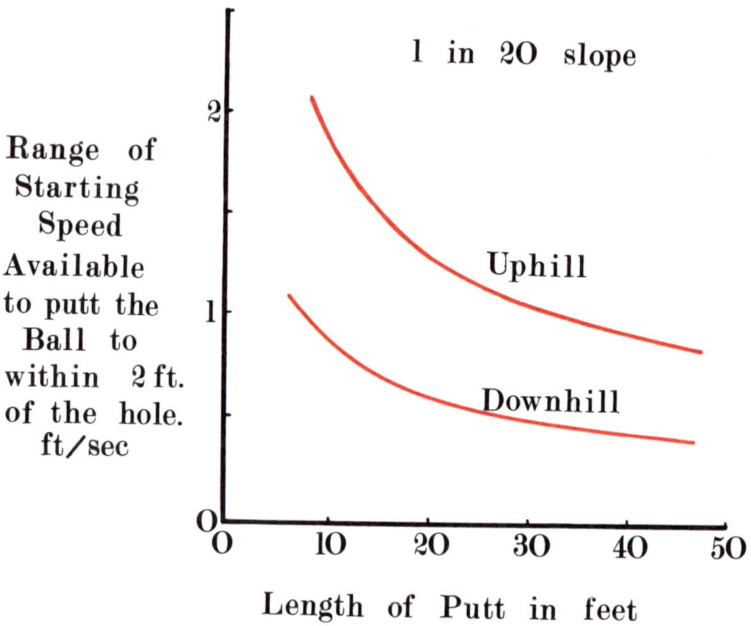


9:3    *The range of starting speeds available to achieve the result of leaving the ball within 2 ft of the hole on a 1 in 20 slope. We have a much smaller margin of error allowable for downhill putts compared with uphill putts, and so they are more difficult.*

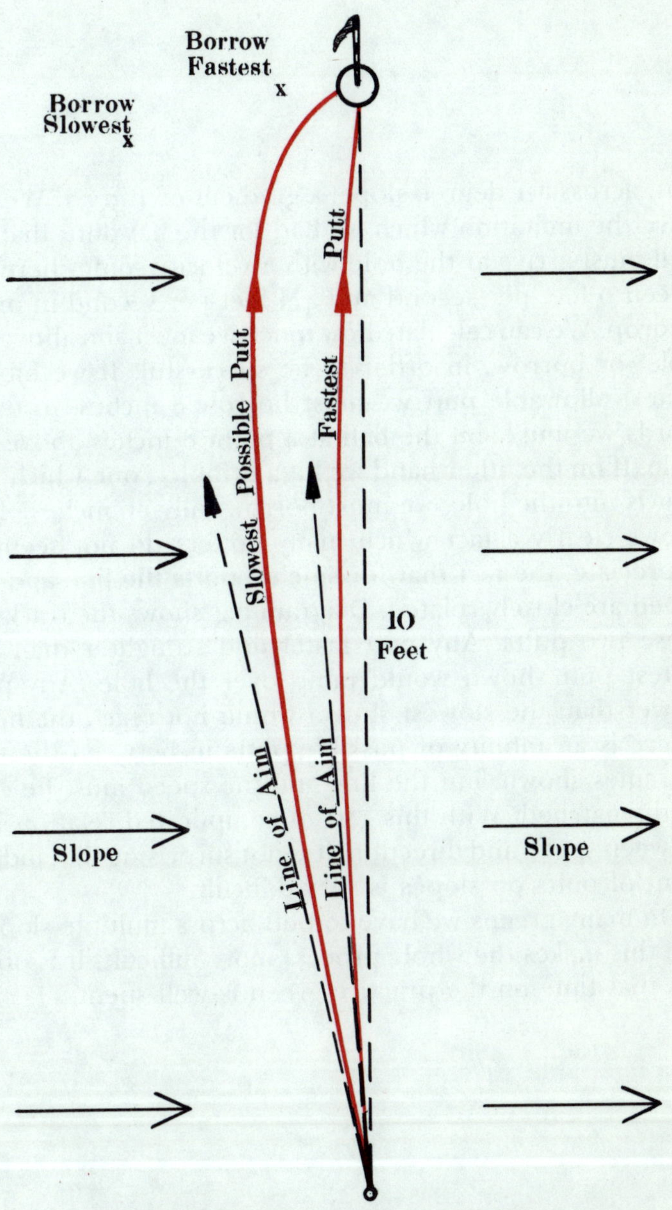


9:4    *A 10 foot putt played across a 1 degree (1 in 57) slope. The fastest possible putt and the slowest possible putt are shown. An infinite number of possible putts exist between these two.*

putt across a 1 degree slope, a gradient of 1 in 57. We still have the limitation which we had for the flat putt, that the ball must arrive at the hole with a velocity somewhere between 0 feet per second and 4.3 feet per second in order to drop. We can calculate how much we must aim above the hole, or borrow, in order to be successful. If we hit the fastest allowable putt we must borrow 8 inches, in other words we must aim the ball at a point 8 inches above the hole. If on the other hand we hit a dribbler, one which just crawls into the hole, we must borrow fully 26 inches. This shows clearly a fact which many golfers do not seem to appreciate, the fact that for sidehill putts the line and the speed are closely related. Diagram 9:4 shows the tracks of these two putts. Any putt faster and straighter than the fastest putt shown would jump over the hole. Any putt slower than the slowest shown would not reach the hole. There is an infinity of possible putts in between the two extremes shown, but the line and the speed must be correctly matched. With this sort of complicated relationship between speed and direction, it is not surprising that judgement of putts on slopes is very difficult.

On many greens we have to putt across multiple slopes, and this makes the whole process more difficult. It is obvious that time on the practice green is well spent.

# 10: Handicap Systems

ONE OF THE ADVANTAGES which golf has over many other games is that players of different ability can play against each other in a moderately satisfactory way. This comes about as a result of the better player giving his opponent a number of shots, this number reflecting the difference in ability. In stroke play competitions, those in which simply the total number of strokes is counted, this is quite satisfactory provided that the players are honest about their handicaps. This is the most common type of competition in the modern game. However, many golfers find Match Play a much more challenging and interesting form of the game. In this type of match each hole is a match in itself, and this provides enormous scope for variation of strategy during the play of a single hole. One of the delights of this game is the way that the advantage can switch from one player to the other so rapidly. It seems to be unpopular with professional golfers, but one of the advantages for the less expert player is the fact that one bad hole does not wreck the entire match, but only results in the loss of that hole. At the end of the round the result is decided by the number of holes won by each player.

There have been many different handicap systems devised for the equalization of abilities in match play competitions. Some of these have been more bizarre than others. One system, called Bowf (Woof in the U.S.), allows an opponent to utter a loud noise like the bark of a dog just at the crucial moment as a player is about to hit the ball. In fact the word is an old Scots word for the bark of a dog. A player is given the right to use the device a specific number of times during a round, and a feeling of apprehension exists at every shot, whether or not the noise actually occurs.

Another interesting handicap system is called 'Yard of

String'. In this, the less able player takes with him a yard of household string and a pair of scissors. The player with the string can elect to receive concessions of distance, without counting a stroke, totalling his one yard during the course of the round. For example, suppose he has a long putt and leaves the ball 6 inches from the hole. He can decide to cut 6 inches from his string and count the long putt as having gone in. Obviously he would only do this if it resulted in a win at that hole. Similarly, if his ball has just trickled into the very edge of a trap so that a 3 inch move would put it onto the fairway, then he can sacrifice 3 inches of his string in order to obtain this improvement without counting a shot. This process continues round the course until all the string has gone. It is surprising how this one yard can make up a difference between two players of quite different ability if it is applied astutely.

The system of 'Bisques' was popular at one time. The bisque was the equivalent of one stroke, and the less able player received an agreed number for the entire round. This number was usually less than the difference in handicaps. The player with the bisques could elect to play them at any hole in the round, and furthermore he did not need to declare the hole until after it had been played; thus he could use one at a halved hole to convert it into a win.

The usual way of applying a handicap is for the players to agree on the number of strokes which one player will receive, related to handicap difference, and then the holes at which these strokes are taken is governed by the stroke index of the course. This means that the strokes are received at the more difficult holes. This is not a very satisfactory system since it attempts to correct a constant difference in ability by means of an incremental allowance. The better player is better on all the holes, not just on the specific holes on which strokes are allowed, although it is true that the difference in scoring is likely to be greater on the more difficult holes. This is probably one reason for the increased popularity of stroke play competitions. However, in changing to stroke play the cut and thrust of match play has been lost. What is needed is a handicap system whereby players of different abilities can compete without the necessity of a stroke allowance, that is on an equal basis on every hole on the course. One way to achieve this would be to play a competition under match play rules with the players each using a different grade of ball appropriate to his ability. The golf balls would still come within the rules of the game, but they would make an allowance for difference in skill.

If we accept this as being a possibility, we can explore the implications in the following way. There are four ways which could be used to provide different grades of golf ball for use in our new type of competition:

1　Variation in the 'compression' of the ball.
2　Variation in the depth of dimples in the surface of the ball.
3　Variation in the diameter of the ball.
4　Variation in the weight of the ball.

Looking at these alternatives, if we used method 1 the less able of the players involved in a match would use a normal, standard ball, while his opponent with his greater ability would use a ball with an appropriately lower compression. This serves to illustrate the principle that the better player accepts a handicap in the form of reduced distance on every shot. Of course, distance is far from being the only factor which separates the expert from the club player, but nevertheless an appropriate reduction in distance would effectively lengthen all the holes, and could go a long way towards compensating for erratic shots, provided they were not too disastrous. This handicap system could never hope to equalise the expert and the rabbit, but for matches between players of not widely different handicaps this could provide the possibility of head-to-head matches.

Method 1 is a possibility, but it has the disadvantage that the grade of a particular ball could not be easily checked, assuming of course that the player does not have available ". . . apparatus approved by the Royal and Ancient".

Method 2 is also possible, since it has been proved by wind tunnel tests that reducing the dimple depth does reduce the lift forces, and hence reduces the length of the drive. However the amount of information which has been published on the effect of dimple depth is so sparse as to make it impossible to predict the effects.

Of the remaining two possible systems, method 4 looks the most promising as an acceptable handicap system. Suppose we could obtain a range of golf balls, in appearance identical to the normal 1.68 inch diameter ball, but with slightly different weights. The advantage of having our computer available to play some shots is that we can carry out an experiment without having to actually produce the balls, and without the uncertainties introduced by human variability. Therefore our expert 'player', who has been hitting all the shots in the earlier chapters, will hit shots with a selection of clubs, using a range of weight-graded golf balls. As before, the woods and medium and long iron shots are played to a firm fairway, providing a good bounce and run. The 9-iron is played to a soft green.

The length of the shots are given in the following table:

| | | | | Distance in Yards | | | | |
|---|---|---|---|---|---|---|---|---|
| Club | 1.62 oz | 1.55 oz | 1.50 oz | 1.45 oz | 1.40 oz | 1.35 oz | 1.30 oz | 1.20 oz |
| 1-wood | 250 | 243 | 238 | 233 | 228 | 223 | 218 | 207 |
| 3-wood | 236 | 228 | 223 | 218 | 214 | 209 | 204 | 195 |
| 2-iron | 211 | 204 | 200 | 195 | 191 | 186 | 181 | 173 |
| 3-iron | 203 | 199 | 195 | 191 | 187 | 183 | 179 | 171 |
| 5-iron | 189 | 184 | 181 | 178 | 174 | 170 | 167 | 159 |
| 6-iron | 171 | 167 | 164 | 160 | 157 | 154 | 150 | 143 |
| 7-iron | 154 | 150 | 148 | 145 | 142 | 139 | 135 | 129 |
| 9-iron | 119 | 118 | 117 | 116 | 113 | 112 | 110 | 104 |

This table of shot lengths clearly shows the expected effect of reducing distance as the ball gets lighter. The variation of distance from club to club closes up slightly as the ball gets lighter. The effect will be similar on any player's game, however far he normally hits the ball. All the golf balls used in this experiment are legal, since the rules stipulate a maximum weight of 1.62 oz.

In order to see how this system would affect club selection we can consider particular examples. Suppose we are standing on the first tee of the Old Course at St. Andrews. The hole which awaits us is 374 yards long, a wide open fairway but with the Swilcan Burn crossing the fairway just at the front of the green. Our expert player, using a standard ball in calm conditions, drives the ball 250 yards down the fairway, and then plays a 9-iron over the burn and onto the green. Now suppose he plays the hole again using a 1.2 ounce ball. This time his drive goes 207 yards, and he is left with a full 4-iron shot. With the burn waiting to gather in any imperfect shot this would be quite difficult to bring off. Using a 1.4 ounce ball, a drive and a 7-iron would be required.

Moving on to the second tee, the standard ball needs a drive and a 6- or 7-iron to cover the 411 yards, whereas the 1.4 ounce ball would require a drive and a 3-iron. The hole would effectively become a par-5 when using the 1.2 ounce ball, being out of reach in two shots.

The longest hole on the Old Course is the fifth, 522 yards, and would require a drive, a 3-wood and a pitch with the standard ball. Using the 1.2 ounce ball, this hole would be a formidable challenge, needing a drive, a 3-wood and a 7-iron.

All these examples show the way that the graded ball would effectively lengthen the hole for the better player. In fact the 1.2 ounce ball would behave in a similar way to the normal ball driven into a 'moderate breeze' of about 14 miles per hour, sufficient to move small branches and raise dust.

One of the advantages of this type of competition would be that the match could be played off the normal tees which were originally designed into the course, thus avoiding the necessity of walking back to tees set further and further back in the trees. So, the poorer player in a particular match would play with the normal standard ball, 1.62 ounce. His more expert opponent would play with a graded ball of weight appropriate to his ability. The course would play more as it was intended to be played, and a match on equal footing as far as strokes are concerned could be played.

The relationship between ball-weight difference and handicap difference between players would have to be established over a period of time in actual play. However, we might surmise that the use of the 1.4 ounce ball might add a shot on every par-5 hole and perhaps add a shot on half the par-4 holes on the course over 400 yards. On this basis the 1.4 ounce ball might add 6 or 7 shots to the round of

an expert player on the present length of course. A return
to the lengths of courses which were common in earlier
times would reduce this back to the standard scratch score.

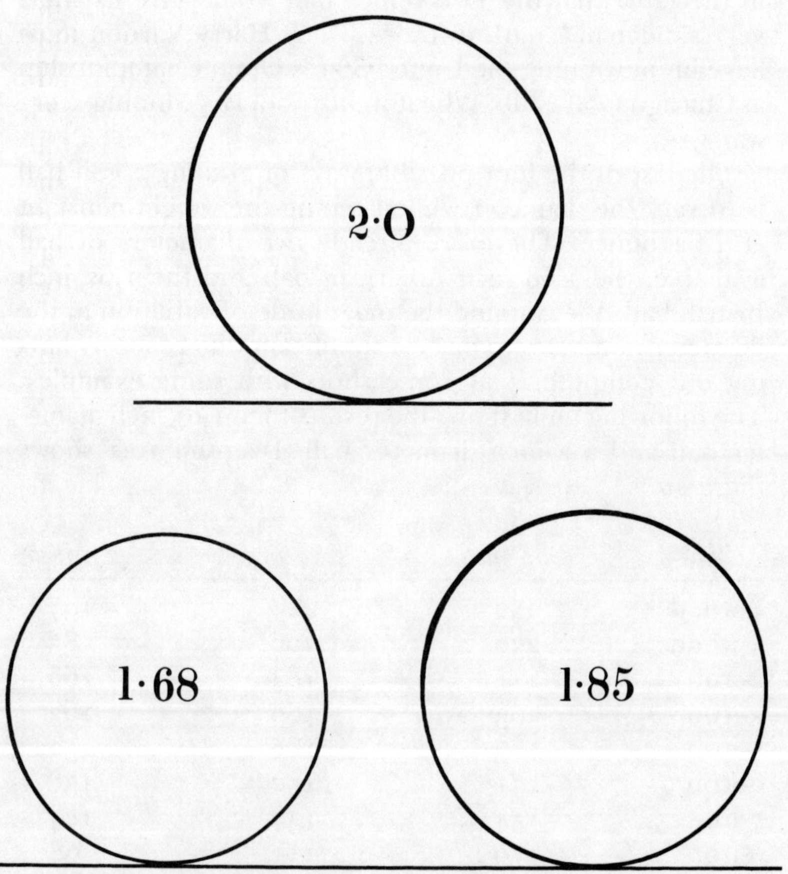

10:1    *Size-graded golf balls. ( 1.68 inches, 1.85 inches and 2.0 inches).*

However, the poorer player, using the normal modern ball, would find his score coming down to the same order. Therefore this handicap system might well make for a very interesting new type of competition to add to all the other types of match which are possible.

It is interesting to notice from the drive lengths shown in the table that the 1.30 ounce ball would give us shots very similar in length to those which Harry Vardon must have hit in winning the United States Open Championship at Chicago Golf Club, Wheaton in 1900. His winning score was 313.

The last of the four possible ways of grading a golf ball is to vary the diameter while keeping the weight constant at 1.62 ounce. There are already two diameters of ball available, the 1.68 inch American ball and the 1.62 inch British ball. We can find the magnitude of variation in the diameter necessary to make a significant difference by having our computer play some shots with some examples. The following table shows the results for a 1.85 inch diameter ball and a 2 inch diameter ball. Diagram 10:1 shows these sizes.

| Club | 1.68 inch | 1.85 inch | 2.0 inch |
| --- | --- | --- | --- |
| 1-wood | 250 | 220 | 197 |
| 3-wood | 236 | 206 | 185 |
| 2-iron | 211 | 184 | 166 |
| 3-iron | 203 | 180 | 162 |
| 5-iron | 189 | 168 | 152 |
| 6-iron | 171 | 152 | 138 |
| 7-iron | 154 | 137 | 124 |
| 9-iron | 119 | 111 | 98 |

Calculations show that a drive with the standard British ball gives a shot 13 yards longer than the drive with the American ball.

While the slightly larger sizes of ball are still within the rules of golf, they are likely to be less acceptable than the graded weight types suggested earlier.

# 11: Odd Shots

One of the advantages of being able to use the computer to play golf shots is that we can examine the effects of some conditions which would be rather hard to achieve in practice.

For example, how would a drive fly if we could put much more backspin onto the ball than normal? If we hit the ball correctly with a driver, the ball takes off with a spin rate of about 57 revolutions per second. We know that as we increase the rate of backspin, the lift force increases. However, this force does not go on increasing indefinitely, but reaches a limiting value. This means that we reach a rate of spin above which there is no further increase in the lift force however fast we spin the ball. If we spin the ball at 300 revolutions per second we will have achieved the maximum possible lift force.

A drive hit with this rate of backspin would, as expected, fly further than a normal drive. The increase in length of carry is 26 yards, 230 yards compared with 204 yards for the normal drive. The rapid backspin causes the ball to stop much more quickly after bouncing, and the total shot ends up at 243 yards compared with 250 yards for the normal drive of our expert. Therefore there would be no point whatsoever in imparting greater backspin to a drive.

The flight path of the shot is interesting, since it shows a slight upward curvature in the early part of the shot. This is because, at this rate of backspin and at high velocity, the lift force is slightly greater than the weight of the ball, so it more than counteracts the force of gravity.

The other extreme is also an interesting shot, and one which every player has managed to achieve at one time or another. This is the drive hit with the sole of the club and dispatched with topspin. It is surprising how many golfers believe that a normal drive has topspin to help it run a long way. In fact this is impossible for any shot hit with an angled face club correctly. However, if we top the ball we can achieve this.

Suppose we hit a drive but, instead of the normal 57 revolutions per second backspin, the ball has 57 revs per second topspin. In this case the Magnus force acts downwards, helping gravity to pull the ball back to earth. So we would expect the ball to dive quickly downwards soon after leaving the club. This is exactly what happens, and although the ball starts off at the normal angle of projection off the tee, the carry is only 112 yards. The ball runs on well, but the total shot is 40 yards short of the normal drive. The side view of the shot is shown in diagram 11:1. Of course the angle of projection of a topped drive is very much a matter of chance, depending as it does on exactly how the sole of the club hits the ball, and many examples observed on the first tee are lower and more depressing than the one shown.

We have seen in earlier chapters how a slice or hook is caused by the backspin being tilted at an angle to the vertical, giving rise to a slight sideways pull in addition to the lift which helps the ball to fly. Suppose we could hit a drive with pure sidespin, could we make the ball "boomerang" and actually start moving back towards the tee? Although in this shot we have maximum sideways pull, we have naturally lost all the upwards lift force, and so a shot started off at the normal angle to the ground, about 14 degrees, would soon dive back to earth, rather in the manner of a shot with no spin. The only way that we might achieve a boomerang shot would be to hit the ball up at a greater angle, in fact at about 40 degrees to the ground. We could then just achieve the shot shown in diagram 11:2. However golf is a difficult enough game without attempting to add this to our armoury of shots.

The angle at which most drives are hit is not necessarily the best from the point of view of achieving the maximum possible distance. If we played a series of drives, each one off a higher tee peg than the one before, in other words with a steadily increasing angle of projection, we produce the shots shown in diagram 11:3. From this we see that the drive hit at an angle of about 20 degrees to the ground would carry the farthest of the shots shown. This is in fact

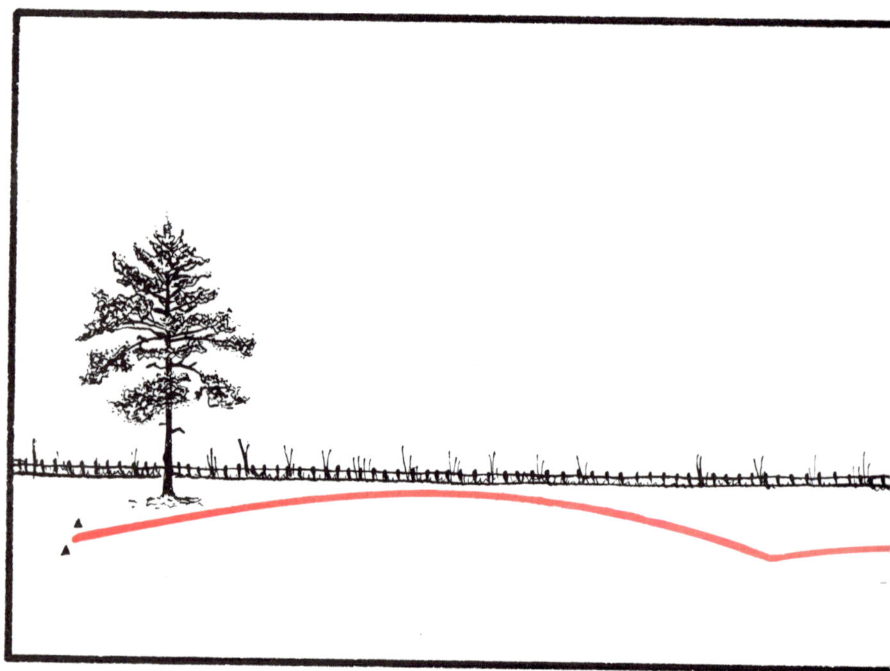

*11:1    The topspin drive, a familiar shot.*

about the best possible angle for a golf drive. The ball bounces and runs on to finish just 8 yards further than the normal drive. The shots at 30 degrees and 40 degrees show a reducing carry and also a shorter run phase because of the steeper approach to the ground. Therefore, although there is a small advantage to be gained from trying to hit more on the up off the tee, the difficulty in doing so more than compensates for the advantage. In order to achieve the 20 degree shot, the point of impact of club on ball would need to be about 3/4 inch above the bottom of the arc of the swing. Allowing for the fact that the bottom of the swing

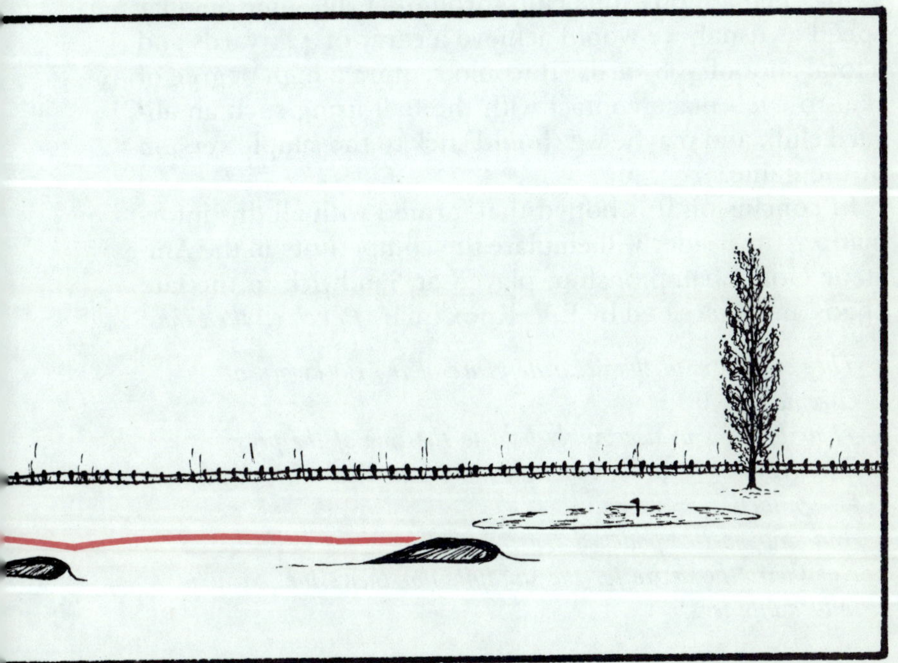

arc would not be right at ground level, this would mean hitting off a fairly high tee peg. If we wished to hit the 40 degree shot shown, we would have to hit the ball off a tee peg at least 10 inches high, a tricky shot indeed.

In the struggle for greater distance off the tee, one way to succeed would be to increase the speed of the club head as it strikes the ball. Assuming that we are already swinging the club as fast as we can, we might consider using a longer shafted club. In order the examine the potential of this approach, suppose we wielded a driver which had, instead of the usual 4 foot shaft, a shaft 8 feet long. If we could swing such a monstrous club through at the same angular speed as usual, we would achieve a carry of 421 yards and a total shot of 468 yards! It would require a high degree of skill to even make contact with the ball using such an absurd club, and maybe we should stick to the simple version of the game.

In conclusion it is hoped that, armed with all this information, the reader will emulate the competitors in the Amateur Golf Championship, played at Sandwich in the late 1920s and described by E.V. Knox in *Mr Punch on the Links:*

*They swung with the accurate grace of the clockwork at Greenwich;*
*Their brassies unswervingly held to the line of the pegs;*
*Their chip shots came down on the greens and mistook them for spinach*
*And stopped like poached eggs;*
*Not theirs the desire for the sandpit, nor theirs the inadequate legs.*

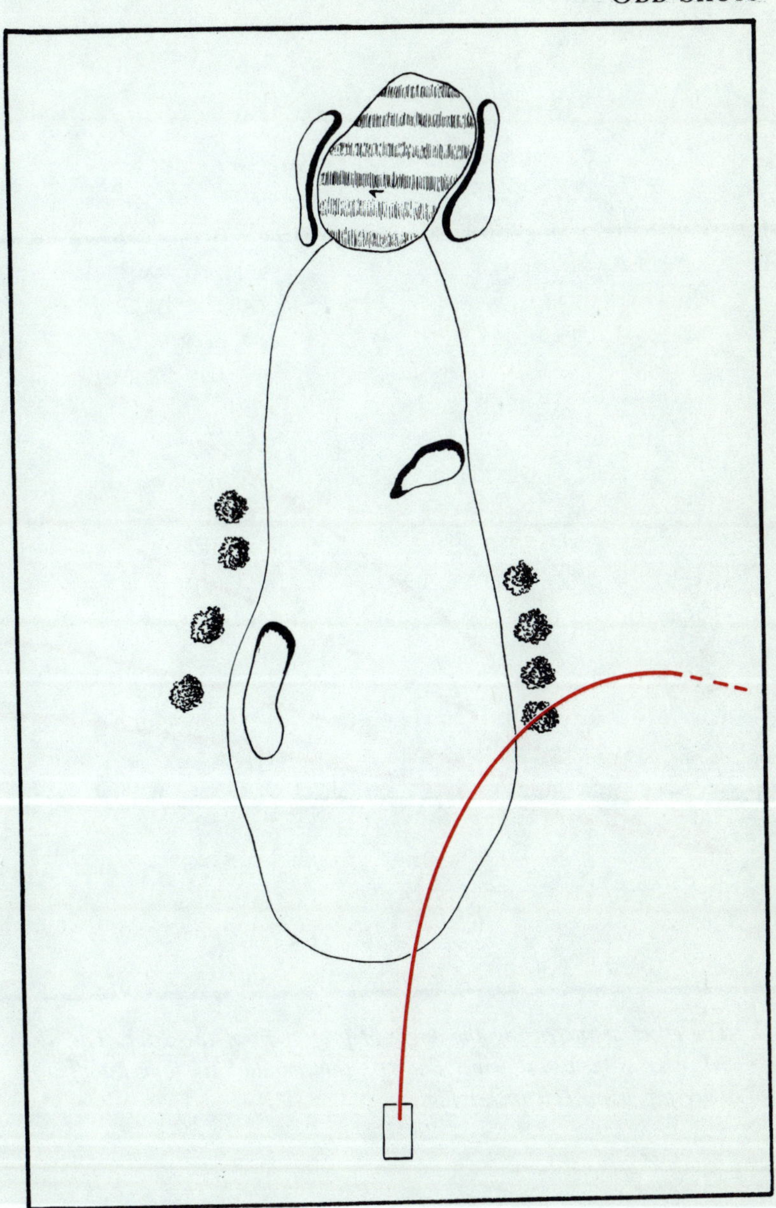

11:2    *A boomerang drive, not easy to achieve.*

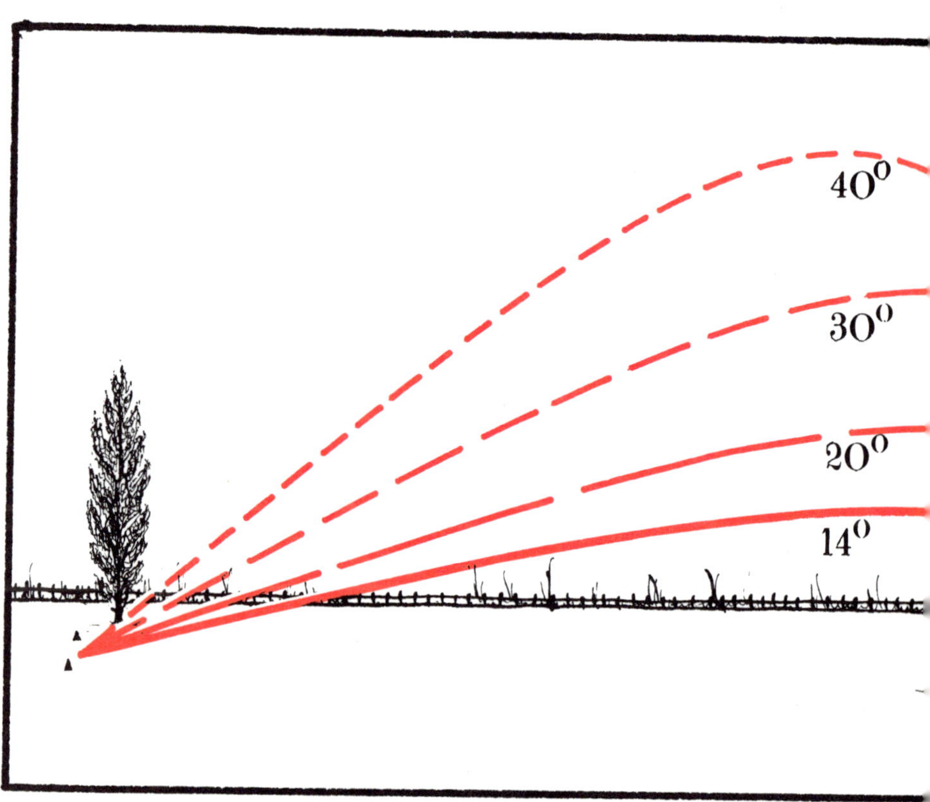



*11:3    The effect of increasing the angle of projection of the drive. The 14° shot is the usual drive. The 40° shot would have to be hit off a tee-peg about 10 inches high.*

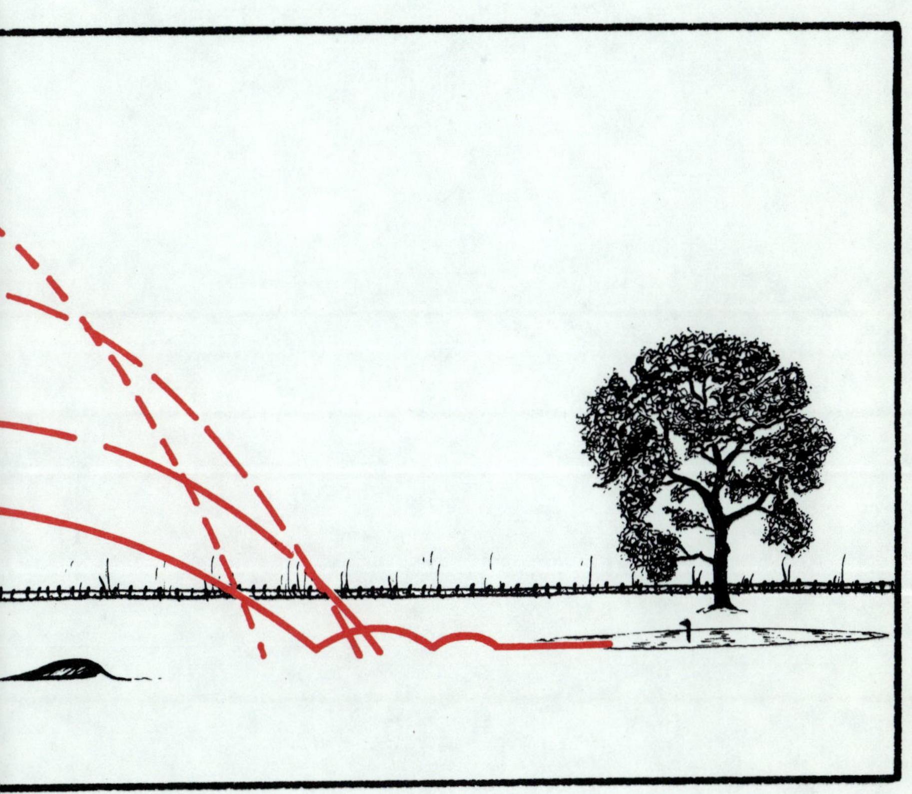

# Bibliography


Anon   *Outdoor Games and Recreations* G.W. Hutchison, Ed., The Religious Tract Society, London (1892) pp 515–18

Briggs, L.J.   *Methods for Measuring the Coefficient of Restitution and the Spin of a Ball,* Journal of Research of the National Bureau of Standards, *34,* 1 (1945)

Briggs, L.J.   *Effect of Spin and Speed on the Lateral Deflection (Curve) of a Baseball; and the Magnus Effect for Smooth Spheres,* American Journal of Physics, *27,* 589 (1959)

Cochran, A. & J. Stobbs   *The Search for the Perfect Swing,* W. Heinemann, London (1968)

Daish, C.B.   *The Physics of Ball Games,* English Universities Press, London (1972)

Daish, C.B.   *Physics and Games,* Bulletin of the Institute of Physics, *15,* 293 (1964)

Davies, J.M.   *The Aerodynamics of Golf Balls,* Journal of Applied Physics, *20,* 821 (1949)

Dobereiner, P.   *The Glorious World of Golf,* Hamlyn, London (1973)

Knox, E.V. Ed.   *Mr Punch on the Links,* Methuen, London (1929)

Lyttleton, R.A.   *The Swing of a Cricket Ball,* Discovery, *18,* 186 (1957)

Newton, Sir Isaac   *New Theory of Light and Colours,* Philosophical Transactions (1672)

Nicklaus, J. & K. Bowden   *Total Golf Techniques,* W. Heinemann, London (1975)

Nicklaus J & K. Bowden   *Golf My Way,* Simon & Schuster, New York (1974)

Scott, T.   *The Observer's Book of Golf,* F. Warne, London (1975)

Tait, P.G.   *Some Points on the Physics of Golf III,* Nature, *48,* 202 (1893)

Tait, P.G.   *On the Path of a Rotating Spherical Projectile,* Transactions of the Royal Society of Edinburgh, *37,* 427 (1893)

Tait, P.G.   *On the Path of a Rotating Spherical Projectile II* Transactions of the Royal Society of Edinburgh, *39,* 491 (1896)

Williams, D.   *Drag Force on a Golf Ball in Flight and its Practical Significance,* Quarterly Journal of Mechanics and Applied Mathematics, *12,* 387 (1959)

# Index